Good Principals Good Schools

A Guide To Evaluating School Leadership

by

Charles H. Slaughter

Foreword by

Wilson C. Riles

LEARNING PUBLICATIONS, INC.
Holmes Beach, Florida

Library of Congress Cataloging-in-Publication Data

Library of Congress Number 88-04500

Slaughter, Charles H., 1929-
Good principals, good schools.

1. School principals—United States—Rating of—
Case studies. I. Title.
LB2831.962.S57 1989 371.2'012 88-45000
ISBN 1-55691-014-2 (pbk.)

Learning Publications, Inc.
P.O. Box 1326, 3008 Ave. C.
Holmes Beach, Florida 34218-1326

Cover Design by Lauren B. Jones

Printing: 1 2 3 4 5 6 7 8 9 Year: 9 0 1 2 3 4

Printed and bound in the United States of America

Acknowledgments

Bill Carey
Thanks Bill.

Garey Morgan
A master teacher.
I appreciate your guidance.

Olive Slaughter
I'm the lucky one. Thank you.

Guadalajara
Un Ciudad Muy Amable.
Muchas Gracias.

To the Reader

This book is written for school superintendents, as a personal guide for developing their own thoughts on the evaluation of school principals. Superintendents may find this book a useful reference to share with board members, particularly those who have a special interest in rating the performance of principals. The book does not speak to a committee, but the contents and activities are appropriate for committee work. It is unrealistic to assume that any responsible administrator, whatever his rank or title, would totally ignore his superiors and subordinates in adopting a personnel evaluation system. It is realistic to expect each individual who is helping to construct an evaluation system to think the job through completely. For that reason, it is strongly recommended that each person who is helping to develop a principal evaluation system should complete each assigned task before the group discusses alternative choices. This does not mean that each committee member must complete all thirty-four tasks before any discussions are held. Rather, it means that each task will be completed by each committee member before that item is discussed in committee.

The advantages of this approach are no doubt obvious; it assures that all parties will do their own thinking before reacting to the discussion; it enhances the probability that all committee members will participate fully, because all have invested something of themselves in the process; and it contributes toward finding and selecting the best choices from the alternatives that the group may develop.

Foreword

In recent years school superintendents have been faced with a virtual avalanche of highly critical reports on the schools. Most of the reports point to problems and shortcomings—of which we are already painfully aware—and with a clarion call to excellence, tell us in general terms "what" ought to be done. They fail, however, to tell school administrators "how" to do it. In other words, school improvement literature today is long on "what" and short on "how".

Charles H. Slaughter's *Good Principals, Good Schools: A Guide To Evaluating School Leadership*, goes a long way toward filling that gap. It is a "how to do it" book that school superintendents seriously committed to school improvement will look at as a useful management tool for use in increasing their effectiveness and in achieving their goals.

The primary focus of the book centers on how to evaluate principals. My own forty years of experience as an educator committed to school improvement has led me to conclude that the primary key to school effectiveness is the principal.

"Show me a good principal and I will show you a good school," is a truism that for years has gone unquestioned. Research on effective schools has only served to validate what experienced observers have always known.

But what are the qualities of a good principal? How do you identify them? How do you evaluate and improve the performance of principals who are already on the job? How do we assist ordinary ones to become good ones? All of the above questions and more have been addressed by Charles H. Slaughter in *Good Principals, Good Schools*.

It is important to point out that Dr. Slaughter speaks not from the viewpoint of a theoretician who occasionally ventures forth from the mountain top of academia to warn of the consequences of our educational misdeeds. His is the voice of a seasoned practitioner drawing from his long and rich experience as an effective teacher, principal, and superintendent. He has put into perspective the purpose of the school as a place to improve and enhance learning.

Dr. Slaughter accepts the idea that school principals are the key to school improvement and outlines methods by which they may be evaluated and assisted to improve their performance. We should be grateful to him for providing us with a guide on which we can rely with confidence as we continue our journey toward educational excellence.

Wilson C. Riles
Former California State Superintendent of Public Schools

TABLE OF CONTENTS

INTRODUCTION

Good Schools and Good Principals

"Goodness" is relative, of course, but by connotation, "good" conveys two meanings simultaneously:

1. Whatever is judged to be good does what it is supposed to do very well, efficiently and effectively, and

2. Whatever is judged to be good is morally and ethically correct.

And so it is with Good Schools and Good Principals: they are more than efficient, more than effective; they are humane and they represent our best.

About the Evaluation of School Principals

Leaders are variously loved and hated, rewarded or abused, praised or condemned, and more. They are tall or short, fat or thin, old or young, masculine or feminine, vain or humble, or somewhere in between the two extremes. Leaders are tough or tender, flexible or firm.

Leadership is society's finest art form: an "Art Form" because its performance eludes the eluctable definitions of science. Its specific acts defy exact reproduction from case to case, and the best performers are so varied in their personal styles.

Management, on the other hand, is something that is studied scientifically, and can be taught as well. Many successful leaders are excellent managers, but not all of them. And excellent managers are not always successful leaders.

Finding an excellent school without a strong leader is a rare occurrence. That person is typically called the principal, but the title doesn't matter. An effective school leader, by any title, sets the school's direction, sets the tone of operations, and supervises the school's operations. A leader gets others to produce results.

In the early eighties, numerous professional journals began publishing studies now known as the "Effective School Studies", which demonstrated the positive relationship between a good school and a competent principal. As early as 1982, K. A. Leithwood and D. J. Montgomery reported on thirty-eight such studies in that year's fall issue of the "Review of Educational Research." Current ERIC listings for "Effective School Studies" must now number in the hundreds. All school administrators are indebted to the scholars who produced those studies. Not that the findings were altogether unknown before the studies became public. The significance was the public credibility given to the studies, and the fact that in them the importance of a school principal's competence was effectively communicated to the public.

The purpose of this book is to provide help for superintendents, legislators, school board members and other interested parties, as they develop or revise a process for evaluating the performance of school principals which will also produce an overall improvement in the schools.

The premise of this book is that evaluating principals for any "fundamental" reason other than to improve a school is misguided, at the very least. Additional reasons for the evaluation of a principal exist, of course, but the position taken here is that school improvement is the primary aim of principal evaluation, and other reasons are secondary to this first concern.

No one principal evaluation system is best. The best systems are tailored to and by the school districts that apply them. As a result, the best systems have integrity, meaning that each evaluation system is unified, complete, and adheres to a common code.

A sound principal evaluation system has five characteristics: it pinpoints principal accountability; it is understandable; it is manageable; it is fair; and it is supported by the members of the school board.

Principal evaluation is often confounded by a desire for conflicting expectations; that is, the evaluation process (or the evaluator) intends to hold the principal accountable for mutually exclusive conditions: such as holding a principal accountable for reducing the school's vandalism according to a prescribed plan and denying the principal the authority to carry out a plan of his or her own. Each evaluation system should recognize that a principal cannot be told exactly "how to do the job" and then be held accountable for specific results. A school environment is in a constant state of flux, and the principal's judgment of the best course of action to produce a desired school outcome may differ from the evaluator's plan of action.

How principals are evaluated will directly influence the actions they take and the decisions they make. Principals are either accountable for what they produce (in results), or they are accountable for the way they perform.

This book outlines a process for developing a Principal Evaluation System which will avoid the error of holding principals accountable for contradictory evaluation standards.

Two critical points of view are constant throughout:

1. The central purpose for evaluating principals is the improvement of schools.

2. The major contradiction found in principal evaluation systems either to hold a principal accountable for school outcomes or to hold the principal accountable for performance objectives must be avoided. The judgment of "principal product" or "principal process" must be undertaken separately and should not be done simultaneously.

How this Book Is Organized

This book presents a thirty-four step process which will guide the development of a principal evaluation system. The process requires the developer's priorities and value judgments to be the basis of the principal evaluation system. It recognizes and allows for tailoring the principal evaluation system according to any special or peculiar local conditions.

Divided into this introduction, ten chapters, and three appendices, the book makes a clear distinction between the evaluation of school principals based on the outcomes they produce and their evaluation in terms of the activities and processes they use in performing their jobs.

Chapter One describes the characteristics of successful principal evaluation systems and identifies the factors which cause evaluation systems to fail. Also, six mandates are given for preparing formal written evaluations of principals.

Chapter Two presents a Case Study which describes a principal and his school. The study is based on real events, with some changes in personalities and setting in order to protect actual people. The study's somewhat atypical school setting is meant to focus attention on the reader's own beliefs and value judgments, and to avoid confusing the concepts it presents with specific particulars of the reader's present associates. The case study provides enough information to show the inherent tug-of-war between judging principals' actions versus judging the results of their work.

The Case Study is the basis for the evaluation exercises, examples and discussions in Chapters Three, Four, Five and Six.

[Note: Every element useful to making a principal evaluation has been selected from the Case Study and is reproduced in a 70 item Data List in Appendix A.]

The narrative story in Chapter Two's case study puts the evaluative data in a human context. However, the reader may elect to not read Chapter Two at all, especially if the reader prefers making principal evaluations from accumulated data rather than from direct observations. All of the necessary data to complete an accumulated data evaluation is contained in The Data List, in Appendix A. (Some superintendents do prefer to evaluate personnel without any consideration of the personalities involved, and if that seems cold-hearted, remember that the Internal Revenue System does this to each of us every year.)

Also, the "raw evaluation data" contained in the Case Study is repeated (as needed) in subsequent chapters.

In **Chapter Three** the development of the principal evaluation system begins with a series of questions the answers for which will reveal the reader's inherent philosophy of principal evaluation. Also presented in Chapter Three is the Data List which is a summary of all of the case study data useful in conducting a principal evaluation. The Data List is also contained in Appendix A. Chapter Three takes the reader through the principal evaluation process leading to a completed evaluation of the case study principal.

Chapter Four presents the philosophy of "Results-based" evaluation. Results-based evaluation focuses on school outcomes rather than administrative process. The rationale for choosing school outcomes as the only fair and rational basis for principal evaluation is presented. Standards for making judgments and sources of evaluative data appropriate to a results-based evaluation system are examined and discussed by the protagonist for this philosophy: Mr. Results.

Following the presentation of the results-based philosophy, an example of results-based principal evaluation is given in the results-based evaluation of the case study principal. This example only uses outcome-type data, taken from the case study. The formal, written results-based evaluation of the case study principal demonstrates that the principal is being held accountable for school outcomes, not for the processes he employs.

Chapter Five follows the same format that was used in Chapter Four. Chapter Five describes a "Performance-based" principal evaluation system. The chapter concludes with an example of performance-based principal evaluation using only performance data taken from the case study. The performance-based evaluator, Mr. Performance, holds the principal accountable for following educational and administrative practices that are generally recognized as valid. School outcomes are not a part of this evaluation.

Chapter Six compares the two principal evaluation systems. It is here that readers are encouraged to compare their own concepts and philosophy of principal evaluation with those presented in the two prototypes by placing their evaluation of the case study principal alongside the two examples and following a step-by-step comparison process. The chapter includes an outline of the steps involved in both of the evaluation processes and a discussion of what was included and/or excluded from each prototype evaluation.

Chapter Seven discusses four management functions: planning, organizing, supervising and controlling, as they relate to systems of principal evaluation. It leads readers through exercises that will serve to make their personally designed principal evaluation systems manageable.

Chapter Eight deals with the need to bring principal evaluation systems into a common focus within the entire school organization, whether that organization is a single school, a large school district, a county-wide school system or any other consortium school organization. The school board and the principals must have confidence in the principal evaluation system; they must participate in the development and execution of the evaluation system to make it work. Chapter Eight describes a process for meeting the need to establish a common focus and includes an exercise which will help the concerned parties to recognize whether or not their principal evaluation process is working as intended.

Chapter Nine discusses the supervision of principals and clarifies the distinctions between evaluation and supervision. Supervision involves directing activities, and it ranges from continuous direct observation (close supervision), to occasional observation (loose supervision) to no observation (indirect supervision). Evaluation, on the other hand, involves judging work performance or work product, rather than directing the worker's actions. Some organizations tie principal supervision and principal evaluation together, while others deliberately keep them apart. The topic of "Dividing Principal Responsibilities" is discussed in this chapter. (The topic deals with any school program that is conducted in the principal's school in which the principal is not directly accountable for the program. In many schools, special education classes are one such example.) The exercises lead evaluators to examine the principal supervision process in their school organization.

Chapter Ten covers principal job descriptions. Readers will learn to write required and useful principal job descriptions that are appropriate to their principal evaluation systems.

Appendix A (as mentioned before) contains the complete Data List taken from the Case Study.

Appendices B and C provide detailed lists of School Outcomes and Performance Evaluation objectives which can be used as guidelines for developing lists of expected outcomes and Principal Performance Objectives.

The development process for the principal evaluation system must follow an orderly process. The steps in the process contained in this book are listed below so that readers will start to become familiar with them and the order in which they occur. The process includes the following 34 Principal Evaluation Tasks:

PRINCIPAL EVALUATION TASKS

1. Identifying School Standards
2. Identifying Principal Accountability
3. Developing Evaluation Criteria
4. Defining Evaluation Criteria
5. Identifying the Data to Be Used in the Evaluation
6. Specifying the Methods of Gathering Data
7. Comparing the Reader's Standards for a Good School with the Case Study School Standards
8. Selecting Data for Use in Making the Case Study Evaluation
9. Ranking the Data in Terms of Its Importance
10. Grouping the Data According to Each Criterion
11. Comparing the Data with the Criteria and Making Judgments

12. Preparing the Final Written Evaluation Document
13. Comparing Readers' Data with Data Used in the Examples
14. Comparing the Findings and Judgments of the Two Examples
15. Comparing Readers' Findings and Judgments with the Two Examples
16. Comparing the Two Evaluators' Recommendations for Action
17. Choosing the Best Approach for Principals
18. Choosing the Best Approach for Students
19. Purposes for Principal Evaluation
20. Written Criteria Definitions
21. Constructing the Data List
22. Listing and Describing Forms
23. Developing Roles
24. Assigning Roles
25. Constructing Time-Lines
26. Training Personnel to Carry Out the Principal Evaluation System
27. Controlling the Principal Evaluation System
28. Techniques to Be Used with the School Board
29. Identifying Rewards for Principals
30. School Board Activities in a Principal Evaluation
31. Principals' Fairness Issues
32. Evaluating the Effectiveness of the Principal Evaluation System
33. Listing Principal Supervisors
34. Writing the Principal Job Description

A Suggestion for Completing the Writing Tasks

The 34 Principal Evaluation writing tasks (PE Tasks), when finished, lead to a complete principal evaluation system. Readers should use whatever writing approach best suits their individual styles for doing these tasks. A plain writing pad, a notebook or a stack of blank cards will do. Some readers will prefer to work at their typewriters or word processors, while others may prefer to tape record their responses or to dictate to their secretaries.

School systems typically develop system-wide programs using committees. Certain assigned individuals complete all of (or portions of) the final written products. If each committee member writes out his or her own individual responses to each PE Task those individuals who produce final documents will have a superior record of each committee member's contributions.

[Note: The advantages of this approach have been well demonstrated through a technique called the "Delphi Method." "Delphi" was invented by the United States Air Force for debriefing bomber crews. Every group has its more outspoken members and many people automatically defer to superiors in group discussions. The best ideas do not always come from either of these types. Delphi insures that all individuals participate and improve the group's results.]

Definitions of Key Words Used in this Book

All personnel evaluation discussions use key words, and even though readers feel confident that they understand the author's meanings, confusion sometimes creeps in. Confusion occurs when more than a single definition to a word exists. Confusion is compounded when an individual or organization adopts a slightly modified meaning to a word. Confusion occurs when we don't know a word's common definition. The reader needs to know exactly what the author intends his words to mean.

This book uses the following words and definitions:

GLOSSARY

Accountable: answerable, responsible.

Administration: the performance of executive duties.

Assumption: the belief that something is true.

Condition: a state of being.

Control: to regulate or guide a system.

Criterion: a standard for making a judgment.

Data: something used as a basis for calculating or measuring.

Direct: to show the way.

Evaluate: to find or fix the value of.

Expectation: the anticipation of something reasonable, due, or necessary.

Fair: marked by impartiality and honesty; just.

Goal: the ideal, or model, toward which effort is directed.

Judge: to form an opinion, or to make an estimate.

Judgment: an opinion, an estimation.

Leader: a person others follow.

Leadership: "the art of getting others to want to do something you are convinced needs doing" (definition attributed to Vance Packard).

Manage: to direct or implement any procedure.

Objective: the aim or end purpose of an action.

Organize: to form separate components into a coherent functioning whole.

Outcome: a result.

Perform: to do in a prescribed manner (as an actor).

Plan: a set of choices designed to achieve a goal.

Procedure: a particular way of accomplishing something.

Process: a prescribed pattern or a procedure.

Program: a plan or combination of procedures.

Purpose: the reason, and intention, for which a thing is done.

Role: the part played by a participant or an actor.

Result: a tangible effect.

Staffing: the assignment of workers to specific positions.

Standard: anything taken as a basis for comparison; a prototype.

Statesman: one who exercises political leadership wisely and without narrow partisanship in the general interest.

Supervision: the direction of the work of subordinates.

System: a regularly interacting group of entities which form a unified whole, such as the operating divisions within an organization.

__tion: a suffix, the result of ______ing.

Value: the worth of something.

1

Personnel Evaluation Systems

Good principals are a superintendent's delight, and the fact is, there are lots of them. Good principals please more than superintendents, though. Students, teachers, staff, parents and school board members admire good principals, as well.

On the other hand, it doesn't take many incompetent principals to make a superintendent's job difficult. A school principal is the operational hand of the entire administrative body. The school board's policy brilliance and the superintendent's management genius amount to nothing without the talents of a competent principal to get the job done in the school.

The late Paul Salmon, former Executive Director of the American Association of School Administrators, was positively ecstatic about the "Effective Schools" studies because they confirmed the fact that a good school depended on a good principal. (1.1) He said, "I've been telling people for years that administrators are important. Now, we have the kind of data that prove it."

The "Effective Schools" studies did something good for principals: They gave principals real recognition, honored their good work, and pointed them in the right directions. These are the same things a Principal Evaluation System should do regularly.

"Principal Evaluation" may be a good conversation topic, sometimes, but in practice it can be an unpleasant thing to do. Superintendents know that behind every personnel evaluation there is a real live person—a person who is sensitive to what is said about him or her, and a person who prefers success to failure. The reality is that no one is successful all the time, and some aren't successful often enough.

Most school system administrators agree that improving personnel evaluation is extremely important, yet, at the same time, it is not something they look forward to doing. Many, many people find principal evaluation a fuzzy topic, full of contradictions and ambiguities. Even though the ultimate purpose of all school personnel evaluation is widely recognized and accepted (to make schools better for students and to improve student learning), implementing a program to improve the process for evaluating school personnel can become so bogged down in argument that the goal seems to be forgotten.

Administrators in school systems re-examine all of their personnel evaluation systems periodically, including the system for evaluating principals. The board may have demanded it; the principals may have protested current practices; the legislature may have mandated it; the superintendent's good judgment may cry out for it; the teachers may clamor for it; the parents may petition for it. None of these demands ever seems to arise at an especially good time. Nevertheless, such demands serve to make such re-examinations inescapable.

Is there ever a good time to revise a principal evaluation program?

Only one thing seems certain: The topic of evaluation does come up. If superintendents take advantage of a period of genuine good will to examine and revise the process, they may risk changing the school system's emotional climate when they do so. Whatever time is selected, they already know that they will encounter some resistance and foot-dragging.

And why should it be otherwise? Aren't there good reasons for educators to find personnel evaluation to be a negative topic? Isn't it true that most employees in most districts find they are not really rewarded for being evaluated, and isn't it also true that personnel evaluation has resulted in some individuals being threatened with severe punishment, such as demotion or firing? From the outset, developing personnel evaluation programs is emotionally-loaded work.

Personnel evaluation systems fail unless the following conditions are observed:

1. The participants must continue to be involved with the system and to support it.
2. Each evaluation must be adapted to a specific individual employee.
3. The aims of the institution must be effectively incorporated within the system.
4. Evaluations must be directed toward job improvement and personal growth.
5. The system must be able to take into account the unexpected or unanticipated.
6. The system must reward excellence as well as criticize sub-standard performance.

Personnel evaluation systems that do survive incorporate certain characteristics:

1. They pinpoint accountability.
2. They are understandable.
3. They are manageable.
4. They are fair.
5. They are supported by the members of the School Board.

Knowing these things makes it possible to develop a Principal Evaluation System that has survival potential.

Mandates for a Principal Evaluation System

Not all personnel evaluation systems are fair. In fact, some seem virtually capricious to the evaluatee. The owner/manager of a small store can fire a clerk in an instant, and that is his prerogative. However, if the clerk is fired without cause, the result may be that the owner/manager must pay the unemployment compensation costs. True, the owner/ manager still has the right to hire and fire whomever, whenever he wants. However, larger organizations and government organizations are held to higher standards for their personnel procedures. Principals cannot be fired summarily. They work under contract, either individual contracts or the employment provisions incorporated into law and policy, and are protected by contract provisions and/or laws and policies.

A personnel evaluation system that is fair and responsible in one person's eyes may not be in those of another. But, personnel evaluation systems must include certain procedural elements to withstand the "standards tests" that higher level employing authorities (and finally the courts) will look for when judging contested cases.

Personnel evaluation systems need to:

1. Describe what is to be evaluated.
2. Determine the evaluative criteria.
3. Determine the data to be used in the evaluation.
4. Specify the methods of gathering the data.
5. Specify who will judge the data in comparison with the criteria.
6. Require a final written evaluation document describing the evaluator's judgments and listing the procedures and actions that will ensue.

Evaluators may prefer to make their own lists of mandates or to make some changes in this list, such as the consolidation of two items or the addition of another. Whatever the change, for whatever purpose, the resulting list will probably still deal with the substance of these mandates. This list of "needs" is in the minds of the those who will be evaluated and in the minds of those who will read and judge the sufficiency of the final evaluation documents. As such, each mandated item compels a thorough and reasoned response.

2

A Principal and His School (A Case Study)

This chapter presents the entire case study that is used as the basis for the evaluation the reader will conduct in Chapter Three.

The case study describes a particular principal, Mr. Swenson, and his school, The International School, located on the high desert somewhere in North America. All of the people and places involved are fictitious. In reality there is no Mr. Swenson and no International School on the high desert of North America, but the story is based on a composite of events that occur in many international schools around the world.

Furthermore, the case study is presented in "faction" form. That is, the "facts" are presented as a "fiction" writer would tell the story. The story is told from the viewpoint of an evaluator of school principals. The evaluator objectively reports what he sees and hears and reserves his judgments about his observations until he writes his evaluation. Individual characters speak in their own voices; their thoughts and words are not "massaged" with qualifying terms that are foreign to normal conversation.

All the necessary information that readers will need to conduct a principal evaluation is contained in the case study. At the end of the study there is a detailed listing of all of the specific data items that an evaluator might use. The same Data List is reproduced in Appendix A.

Some evaluators prefer to evaluate personnel from collected data lists rather than through direct observation. And other evaluators with special interests in evaluating principals, such as school board members and superintendents in large school systems, sometimes are precluded from conducting their own direct observations. Readers who belong to one of these categories may elect to bypass this chapter, go directly to Chapter Three and use its Data List for completing the evaluation exercises.

The Case Study—Background

The school is seven years old, located on a barren plateau in western North America. It is here because of a project being conducted by the government of the United States and several other friendly nations who share a common problem and have a common need. The people who work in this community are water specialists who find water where it does not appear to exist and clean it up when it is rotten. They are scientists, technicians, and laborers. The majority are employed by their respective European, Asian, African, and Middle Eastern governments; with U.S. citizens constituting the majority. A few of the Americans are employed by two private corporations. They live in this remote location because solving the water problems here will lead to similar solutions in desert areas on every continent.

A school was built for the children of all of the workers because they demanded that their families stay together. The school is named "The International School," but it has an American curriculum and a traditional American approach to schooling for all of its students, more than half of whom are U.S. citizens with the remainder coming from more than a dozen other nations.

The school is headed by the principal and operated under a private contract with a small corporation (which also is headed by the principal). Under the terms of the contract, the school will operate a mainstream U.S. public school program designed to keep students at their regularly expected achievement and performance levels.

Most of the school's funds come from the United States government, but the only U.S. government involvement in the school's business operation is in maintaining the contract. Therefore, once a year a U.S. official visits the school to see that the contract's conditions are being carried out. Should problems regarding the quality of the school's education program arise, the government must send an outside evaluator to evaluate the situation and make recommendations. Allegations have been made that educational problems do exist; therefore, an outside evaluator has been assigned to visit the school.

The Case Study Scenario

Today an evaluator is visiting the school. He is an experienced educational administrator employed by the U.S. government and he is there to evaluate the school and write a report of his findings. It seems that someone thinks this is not a good school and has said so in high places. Even in this school, especially constructed for a diverse international community and located on a remote North American high desert plain, an American parent has decided to exercise his basic right to complain about his child's schooling.

According to the terms of employment, all children of U.S. government employees are entitled to a free education that meets American standards. If a public school is not available, a private one must be provided. If the private school is inferior, then the cost of a private boarding school elsewhere must be paid by the employer. In instances where there are numerous students but no private school is available, the U.S. will open a school of its own. The decision as to which of these types of schools, or education, the government will give its support is finally determined by the expense involved. The choice that the government makes will be the option that will meet educational standards at lowest cost.

The Physical Plant

The Spanish arches that line the school's wide exterior corridors are unusual to school construction but attractive. The single story building, made of thick adobe with small windows, is clean and litter free. The surrounding playground is raw dirt and rock, ungraded and uneven. Two meager basketball standards, the only permanent playground equipment, leave the impression of being bent, when in fact they are not.

An open courtyard, covered with decorative tile, separates the classroom pods from the office building. The courtyard's morning function is to serve as the gathering and greeting place for the students, staff and the day's regular contingent of parent volunteers. This morning there is also a visitor: the evaluator.

Staff and Students

Two hundred students and twenty-five staff members arrive every morning via an assortment of vehicles, from limousines to battered cars. There are no buses. The school's enrollment and staff size remain virtually the same from year to year because the water project (which is the reason for all the people being here) always has roughly the same number of employees.

The Evaluator's Observations of the School Day

Mr. Swenson, principal of the school, stands center court giving greetings. He has been away for awhile making arrangements for new program materials and staff in-service, and he is obviously very happy to be home. A special warmth can be detected in each "Good Morning," and he always has the right name to go with the greeting. There is no dawdling along; adults and youngsters alike move with a sense of purpose. They are going to work.

The daily activities continue in the same way that they began: people moving about, working, studying, always friendly, and always with a sense of purpose. The pattern continues throughout the school day. The teachers act with obvious purpose, and the students certainly look like they are learning.

The Evaluator's Observations of Parent Opinions

The informal conversations in a series of evening cocktail parties reveal that parents think their children are learning at school. But there is another message in those conversations as well: the school is in conflict. The people at each cocktail party have a different interpretation as to why this is so.

The Europeans are somewhat startled, in a state of dignified and restrained disgust for the critical outburst that was made by some of the Americans. They have elected this American style school experience for their children and are grateful that the opportunity is available. All too soon, their youngsters will return to the traditional educational rigors in their native countries. What do they like about this school? "Just look at the children," they say. "They are happy and having a good time learning. What you see speaks for itself."

The Middle Eastern adults are outraged: "Don't those complaining fools know that they are endangering the whole school?" For them, this American education experience is their children's only opportunity for a real education.

The Americans size up the situation this way: the number of critics is small. Tom Brown, a senior U.S. project administrator, is the spokesman. His small support group has left him to hold the bag while they remain silent. The majority of Americans have a consensus solution: punish the critics with traditional American dignified censure (ostracize them). Then, use the opportunity to promote modest reforms. The American majority wants a school advisory board to review and advise the annual budget. Further, they want standardized achievement tests, at least for the American students. (The Europeans will tolerate the testing nonsense as long as their own children are not involved. They ask, "Don't the teachers already know how well their students are doing?")

The visiting evaluator met with Tom Brown the second day of his visit. Mr. Brown's enormous office, with a large walnut desk, a rich conference table for six and a conversation area, furnished with a plush upholstered couch and chairs of soft brown leather, reflected his rank. He greeted his guest formally and began talking as they sat down.

Tom said he knew that his cause was unpopular, but he also knew he was not alone. "Projects like ours depend on bringing high quality personnel to a God-forsaken part of the world. People will come for better pay, advancement opportunity and recognition in their own fields. And their spouses and children will only come if the school is good. But company personnel won't come without their families. The word goes out—on how good things are here—to the families that we try to recruit as replacements in the coming years. My professional concern is in keeping a steady flow of competent workers on this project."

As he spoke, the evaluator took measure of Tom Brown: Ivy League by his appearance. His voice had a defensive ring.

"I sent my own son home to Arizona to attend school there rather than risk educating him here," Brown said.

Brown seemed to recognize from the evaluator's attentiveness that he was being listened to. He began to make more eye contact; his confidence grew.

"People seem to think that I'm out to get John Swenson. I'm not. I do think he hires too many people from the church he belongs to."

"That could be serious," said the evaluator. "Do you have any data to support your impression?"

"I have no evidence that any of them bring their religion into the classroom, but those are subtle matters. A parent seldom hears anything about such things until it is too late. In a place like this, we expect teachers to be involved in many after school activities with kids. They have more than the ordinary amount of time with their students. I'm not saying there is any religious indoctrination. It's just that it would be too easy to do it without being caught."

"Are there problems that you do have evidence for?"

"The school needs athletic equipment and playground equipment. Our youngsters don't have opportunities for Little League and the other organized sports that they have at home. These kids need experiences like that to help them grow up American."

(Tom Brown's self assurance increased as he spoke about concrete things.)

"Swenson bought personal-sized computers before addressing more important needs. I'm not against computers; I'm a scientist. I am against his priorities. He has hired a seventh and eighth grade science teacher with no training for the job. I can see such a person teaching science in the lower grades, but at the junior high level science is tougher and requires a qualified teacher. He should have located someone with at least a couple of more advanced college science courses."

The evaluator then asked Tom Brown to tell him about his son's experience in the school.

"My son's school experience last year was a disaster. He had an outright incompetent teacher who could not maintain order. The students made fun of him and he fell to their level. Yet, Mr. Swenson defended him. He also told me it cost a lot of money to recruit teachers for this location and he didn't have a lot of money to spend. A competent administrator would budget a reserve to deal with such a problem. Anyone can make a bad decision, he should expect to make some, but good teachers are the most important thing he can bring to this school. If you have someone teaching who is a clear detriment to students, you have to get rid of him."

"Didn't other parents complain?"

"They complained, but most accepted Swenson's explanation. I don't know why he always sounds so short of funds. Each child's education here is supported by his nations' government, or by his parents' employer, and both pay the bills that are sent. Swenson is provided housing as a part of his contract, and the cost of house improvements and repairs is a part of the school's expense. Have you seen the house he had built? It is more house than what you see here, except for the

chief administrator's house, and the chief does considerable entertaining, something John Swenson never does."

"Your son is back in Arizona now, and you have little contact with the school this year; do you have any assessment of how things are in the school today?"

"I understand that some things may be improved," Brown replied. *"I know the most incompetent teacher is gone, but the science teacher is still there. I made a lot of people unhappy by voicing my concerns. Many of the mothers are afraid a bad report on the school will lead to its closing, and they want to keep their families together."*

He paused for a drink of water, took a single swallow, and said,

"I am the guy the critics talk to out of fear of speaking up themselves. I hear from many parents that they do appreciate what I did. They share my concerns for the school, and they know there are alternatives to closing the school. I can give you their names if you insist, but it's better not to. This is a small community and people have to try to get along."

Evaluator's Observations of the Swenson House

The evaluator thanked Brown and returned to the school. He drove by the Swenson home on his way back to the school. The house was much more impressive than others in the area. He spent the next day and a half in the school and close to John Swenson.

Evaluator's Observations about John Swenson

Swenson is an unusual man, a bit eccentric in fact. He is completely at home in a place that most people are anxious to leave. All the people working here enjoy the high pay, but, for Swenson, making money is so important that he has made every imaginable mental compromise, to the point that he now considers this the ideal life.

Dress him up in regular business attire and he wouldn't look the least bit unusual. He is just over five feet six inches tall, trim and fit. When he smiles he seems to show all thirty- two teeth. His wardrobe came from the racks of any discount store. He bought fifteen dollar polyester slacks when they went on sale for five. His wife cuts his straight black hair (not at all well) and he drives a small Japanese pickup. His annual income is not known because the school is owned by a small corporation which is in turn owned by Swenson, his immediate family and one or two friends.

Besides knowing a great deal about teaching English Literature, John is competent in developing a sound basic skills program. He is an enthusiastic disciple of Mastery Learning, with its concepts of clearly stated objectives, regular testing, and student feed-back. He is both intelligent enough and knowledgeable enough to run a good elementary school. His social skills dictate that it be far off the beaten track. His recruiting skills demand that the school have a built-in supply of competent teachers. John is one of those unusual personalities whose talents only flourish in a non-standard environment.

What the Evaluator Learned about Swenson's Professional Background

John's career began by teaching high school English in Montana. He left before getting tenure and started teaching in a series of overseas schools in obscure outposts. While most Americans could put up with these assignments for two to four years before abandoning the high pay in order to regain their sanity in another, more homelike environment, Swenson loved it. His dream was to operate his own school and live the life of a colonial potentate. A couple of summers in the States and he earned a Master's degree in school administration. He had two interim administrative assignments before reaching his goal: one was on a Nepalese mountain and the other in Zaire.

Evaluator's Personal Acquaintance with John Swenson

The evaluator had first met Swenson at an international administrators conference in San Francisco. While the conferees registered at the conference hotel, Swenson went to the YMCA. The other administrators kidded him about his never buying tickets to the cocktail parties, yet always attending them. He had an uncanny ability for finding the person with a ticket who was not going to attend.

Swenson had asked the evaluator for help in finding a consultant to come conduct an in-service program in Mastery Learning techniques for the school staff.

Evaluator's Interview and Observations of John Swenson

The evaluator went to John's office for a confidential interview. Unusual items in an otherwise Spartan office were a remarkably expensive personal computer and expensive state-of-the-art laser printer, and a giant-screen television with two VCR's.

The evaluator spoke first.

"John, my job is to get at the issues, and frankly I don't think Tom Brown is an issue. Neither does he think you are an issue. He thinks the issues are: first, a religious imbalance in the staff; second, an unqualified person teaching upper grade science; third, buying twenty personal computers while physical education equipment and after school programs are inadequate; fourth, failure to budget funds for a realistic - contingency, such as the midyear dismissal of an incompetent teacher; and fifth, excessive use of school funds to develop your residence. Beyond these points, your supporters are concerned about a lack of standardized testing and your perceived unwillingness to accept advice. I want to hear your side of these criticisms."

John Swenson sat straight up in his chrome and naugahyde office chair. His eyes never left the visitor, and his stiff posture never changed.

The evaluator went on.

"Let's start with the last point, John. What are your views on seeking, and accepting, advice from parents and staff?"

"My contract is clear, I am in charge of the school. I want good advice, but not from just anyone; I ask for it from the people I have confidence in."

"What about the demand for a testing program?"

"I'm willing to install a testing program, at least for the American students. Our students are all working above grade level in their textbooks, so I don't see why we should spend money on extra tests. We do not accept students who cannot function in a regular program. The project directors and the personnel officers know that. Families with handicapped children do not come here, as you know."

"Yes, I know that, John. Tell me something about your priorities and how you budget for them."

"I have saved this school thousands of dollars. No one could be more conscientious about thrift, but I am not about to relinquish my authority over the budget. I normally review my budget with the project comptroller to see if my costs fall in line with theirs. Educational priorities are my area of expertise. The school does need more physical education equipment, and we should get some of it within a year."

"What do you say to the criticism about buying computers before taking care of the other needs?"

"We have an academic program and the computers are in keeping with that program. We obtain hundreds of pieces of free software from the public domain market. Two of our teachers have made considerable use of the computers for a variety of things. Their students all make use of software programs at least twice a week."

The evaluator interrupted with another question.

"Do you have plans to integrate the computers into your regular program or have you developed a program which requires computers?"

"The third and fifth grade teachers are making the most use of our computers right now. We will expand computer use next year."

"That sounds like a good idea John, especially if you can integrate computer use within an educational plan. Now, about that really bad teacher you had here. Why didn't you replace him midyear?"

"Now, let me tell you something about contingency budgeting. We do have a small reserve, but setting aside thousands of dollars each year to deal with an unlikely contingency is robbing the school program. We need all the money we get. The teacher in question was not the best teacher we had. Actually, he was a poor teacher. He left at the end of last year of his own accord. Doesn't just about every school have at least one poor teacher?"

"You miss the point John, everyone picks up a very poor teacher now and then; they don't always hold on to them. Let's leave that. What about the concern for upper grade science?"

"As for the science teacher, they are hard to find. Miss Goode has a life-long interest in science. She is not formally well-trained, but she has prepared herself. She is certified, to teach music."

"John, how do you react to the charge that there is religious imbalance on your faculty?"

"The attack on my religion is nothing more than a slur. You have met my fourteen professional staff members of whom eleven are regular classroom teachers, and, of those, eight are the wives of men working for the project. The other six staff members, three teachers and three other staff positions, are actually three married couples. The Johansens came here first and they helped recruit the other two couples. Is it unnatural that their friends might be from the same faith?" Somewhat angrily he asked, *"Have I left anything out?"*

The evaluator wasn't disposed to have John angry, but he could handle it. He asked his last question.

"Can you respond to the concern about diverting funds into your personal residence? And for my own benefit, you seem to have more high quality electronic equipment in your office than most school administrators. How do you use it?"

There was a pause while Swenson regained his composure.

"Most families are here two years, a few stay three years, and only senior project administrators stay four. My family and I are here for the duration of the project. This is our only home and we expect to live in comfortable housing. The equipment you mention is useful in my work."

Swenson seemed genuinely perplexed that anyone could find anything serious to negatively criticize in the school. He completely reduced those criticisms that existed (and he knew them all) to the status of a crank's trivial carping.

Evaluator's Final Observations

So there it is. Mr. Swenson had an answer for each complaint. Classroom visits and a series of staff interviews support the claim of high student achievement. The majority of teachers have been away from the regular U.S. public schools for only one or two years and they say these students are typically above average performers. The upper grade science program is of a lower standard than the rest of the academic program. Non academics (physical education, art, and music) have low priorities. Not a single course that could be called a "frill" is offered. The high level of common understanding and acceptance of the school's academic goals is exceptional. The school operates in an atmosphere free of conflict. There is no record of serious accidents (very few scraped knees, even, in spite of the undeveloped playground). A few teachers complain privately that they work much harder here than in their previous jobs. They do not take their concerns to Swenson because he does not understand the meaning of not working to capacity. They have not requested additional instructional materials, but in fairness to the staff, they are resourceful and used to making do. Those who hint at Swenson's eccentricities are quick to say that any other principal would find it difficult to operate a school like theirs. Do they like him? That is not clear. They do respect him. If he were a bit more approachable he would have some close friends (in the traditional meaning of the term) but Swenson doesn't seem to need close friends. He might well describe friendly acquaintances as close friends.

Epilogue

On day three the evaluator left to prepare his written evaluation. His recommendation would cause one of the following things to happen to John Swenson:

1. the presentation of a bonus for operating a superior school;
2. nothing at all;
3. censure for his poor performance in certain areas which could include withholding some funding;
4. allowing the school to continue operation only with a change of administrator;
5. termination of the school's contract with John Swenson's corporation.

To the Reader

Bearing all these observations and particulars in mind, how would you go about evaluating John Swenson, school principal, and his school?

3

A Step-By-Step Development of a Principal Evaluation Document

One purpose of a Principal Evaluation is to use it to identify and then upgrade, reinforce or change a principal's behavioral practices in order to benefit students. A second purpose for the evaluation is to benefit the principal who is evaluated; to point out the positives and negatives, if any, for purposes of improvement. Still others (teachers, parents, the community at large) also may benefit from the results of the evaluation because of the changes that the principal may make after the evaluation.

Principals will benefit by being recognized and rewarded for their good work, and by being given the opportunity to improve their work wherever improvement is needed. On the down side, those principals who demonstrate an inability to do their jobs well and fail to improve, as needed, should be reassigned.

There are numerous tasks with which evaluators must deal in order to formulate viable principal evaluation systems for use in their own schools. This chapter presents twelve Principal Evaluation Tasks (PE Tasks) for readers to consider. Readers are urged to carefully examine each PE Task and to provide written responses to its particulars. (Readers may want to review the suggestions for completing the writing tasks that were given in the Introduction.)

PE Task 1: Identifying School Standards

Answer this question: what conditions should exist in a good school? The answers may include specifics never found in a school, but which are the achievement of things that should be the goals of a good school (for example, all students should be reading at a level equal to their abilities; no vandalism; no serious student injuries)—all the conditions the reader would expect to find in a good school.

Many school administrators and school systems have already determined their standards and written them in the form of statements. School standard statements represent the levels of performance or achievement that must be met or surpassed within a given school (or school system). Anything less than the standard is not good enough. A typical school standard might be: "All students will pass the school system's minimum proficiency examinations with eighty percent correct answers."

In addition, many school systems have formulated goal statements which present performance levels that go beyond their system's standards. Goal statements describe ultimate aspirations. A typical goal statement might be: "All students will develop an appreciation for great literature."

Many goal statements are unattainable. They describe ideals that cannot serve as a solid realistic basis for accountability. Even so, stated goals, however lofty, do serve a practical purpose. They set the directions toward which responsible schools should aspire and toward which responsible school principals should aspire, as well.

DO PE TASK 1 NOW

As an opening exercise, readers should write a comprehensive list of what they believe to be important standards in any good school. Next, readers should rank each item according to its priority, from most to least important.

[Note: Do not be concerned with the principal in the case study at this point. The first steps in developing a Principal Evaluation System are based on the developer's basic values, not on a particular individual who is to be evaluated.]

PE Task 2: Identifying Principal Accountability

Answer this question: For what should principals be held accountable? Is it their responsibility to cause the school to achieve the standards that were identified in PE Task 1? Are principals to be held accountable for their schools' outcomes, such as student test scores? Are principals to be held accountable for the processes they follow, such as holding regular staff development meetings? Are they to be held accountable for specific functions, such as personnel evaluation? Or are principals accountable for some of each?

DO PE TASK 2 NOW

Write a concept statement encompassing all of the responsibility areas for which any school principal should be accountable. Keep the concept statement as simple as possible and the rest of the process will be more manageable.

Items in the principal accountability list may be stated as a single word, a short list of words or a simple statement. A suitable answer might be: "(I believe) principals are responsible for being strong educational leaders in their schools."

Writing the principal's accountability concept statement represents the first big step in the process of developing a customized principal evaluation system. It captures the field of information which will be used in a formal evaluation document.

Having completed the first two PE Tasks, identifying both the standards of a good school and the characteristics of a principal's accountability, reader-evaluators have created a basic pool of concepts from which to further develop and refine their individual principal evaluation systems.

PE Task 3: Developing Evaluation Criteria

The next step is to classify components of the principal accountability statement list into like categories, again in general terms. (In a subsequent PE Task, the general terms developed in this current task will be used to identify specific evaluative elements).

For example, the principal accountability statement (in PE Task 2), "(I believe) principals are responsible for being strong educational leaders in their schools," could serve as a criteria category under which readers/evaluators should list those qualities associated with being a strong educational leader.

Readers/evaluators who are "management" oriented may develop categories according to the principal's job functions (staff training, curriculum management, budgeting and others). In this situation, the readers will list the things they associate with being a strong educational leader. These might include such items as:

- management competency
- communications effectiveness
- morale level
- student achievement level

Readers/evaluators who are looking for "school outcomes" may want to list categories that repeat the school standards developed in PE Task 1. Such evaluators may want to focus on the principal's school level responsibilities (student achievement, school safety) and perhaps one or two categories that focus on the principal's district level responsibilities (the principal's responsibilities as a spokesperson for the district).

Readers/evaluators whose focus is on how principals "perform their roles" will develop performance categories (leadership, management and others).

Constructing the list of categories is a step which gives individual names, or titles, to the criteria that will be used in writing the Principal Evaluation System Document.

Readers/evaluators should be sure to include headings that embrace every characteristic known to be important in a good principal. For example, many evaluation systems make no specific reference to honesty, per se, but principals work under a contract, and honesty is expected with regard to written contracts. Otherwise, contracts wouldn't work and the law presumes a basic level of honesty between contracting parties.

One way to specify a criterion that includes the honesty concept is:

"Fully complies with all contract expectations."

Readers can use the previous statement as a model for writing a criterion statement for each category of principal accountability.

DO PE TASK 3 NOW

Readers should write down the names or titles of criteria for evaluating a school principal.

PE Task 4: Defining Evaluation Criteria

Having named the criteria, the next step is to thoroughly define each of them; to identify the specifics to be evaluated; and to state exactly what is to be expected of principals. The "expectation" part is critical because it specifies the job standards against which principal performance will be judged.

In PE Task 3 "management competency" was listed as an example of a criterion. A definition of management competency should include all aspects of management that apply to a principal. Since "budgeting" is one aspect of management, the expectation might read:

"produces good budgets" or

"follows good budgeting practices."

However, these standards are not specific enough, because the word "good" has no firm meaning. Therefore, the expectation should be more specific, such as:

"doesn't exceed budget," or

"constructs budgets in sufficient detail to follow expenditures closely."

DO PE TASK 4 NOW

Because defining criteria takes more time than readers may care to invest right now, write only as many examples as desired. Later in the book, PE Task 20 will take readers into more detail on this topic.

PE Task 5: Identifying the Data to Be Used in the Evaluation

Having specified the principal's job standards as accountability categories, listed the criteria, and defined them as expectation statements, there now needs to be a list of data for use in making the principal evaluation system document. (Some criteria may already name the data for making the evaluation, but not all criteria do this.) Specifying the evaluation data is an important but time consuming task.

[Note: in the interest of time, the reader may want to pass this task over for the moment because the data needed to evaluate the case study principal, Mr. Swenson, is already provided in the data list. Later (in PE Task 21), this same topic, "Identifying the Data to be Used in the Evaluation," will be addressed in detail.]

All evaluators use data of some kind to form their judgments; even what they have in their heads is data. But, because this kind of information is so totally subjective, it is hardly the kind of data that should be applied to personnel evaluations.

Trying to identify all the data for use in evaluating principals, before beginning the evaluations, could take forever unless some general data classifications are employed. In the criterion example, "management competency," data might include:

1. all management documents
2. all management reports
3. all management observations
4. any other management related data the evaluator finds useful

Using this brief list, superintendents who are concerned about budgets have access to all budget data for carrying out their principal evaluations, because budgets are management documents. This list should include all the budgets, budget reports, budget meeting minutes, budget memos, and budget rumors.

Evaluators are advised to include open-ended items (such as item 4, above) because doing so allows them to use any resource that they consider relevant to their task. As a practical matter, judges do that anyway. There is no way to get inside a judge's head and limit what he or she uses in making a judgment. (For example, a highly sensitive bit of information concerning a negative aspect of a principal's ethical or moral conduct may come to a superintendent in an extremely confidential manner. The superintendent would be unwise to judge the principal without more data. However, the report is one piece of data, and it should not be ignored.)

If the evaluators use anything they choose, why bother making a data list? The answer is: The Third Party, a very important person, whom many evaluators unfortunately fail to fully consider. The final written evaluation exists for a third party to review, and the third party will judge its sufficiency.

If the written evaluation fails to identify the evidence used in its preparation (the data) and fails to link "relevant data" with its "conclusions and judgments," it may not be sufficient to pass the third party's standards of expectation.

DO PE TASK 5 NOW

Readers should make a list of the types of data necessary for making a principal evaluation. Because this topic will be readdressed in greater detail during PE Task 21, readers should list as many examples as they wish, for now.

PE Task 6: Specifying the Methods of Gathering Data

Having determined the types of data needed for making a principal evaluation, it is now time to specify the methods that will be used to gather it.

1. In one method the evaluator gathers and collects all the data himself. In school systems where this approach to principal evaluation has been established, a common handbook will describe the data gathering procedures that the evaluator will use, be they direct observations, a series of reports, meetings or whatever.

2. A second principal evaluation system method will provide that all principal evaluation data be sent to the evaluator. Some sort of principal evaluations system handbook will specify who will send which data to the evaluator, and when.

3. A third (and more common) variation combines the previous two. The combined method will also rely on a handbook of principal evaluation system procedures to specify all of the various options evaluators may use for gathering principal evaluation data.

[Note: "gathering data," like "specifying data" will be discussed again in a later chapter. For the moment, remember that written evaluations exist for a "third party review," and gathering data involves a "fairness" concept that is pertinent to all evaluation activities.]

DO PE TASK 6 NOW

In the interest of time, readers should list one to three data gathering methods they will want to include in their principal evaluation systems.

PE Task 7: Comparing the Readers' Standards for a Good School with the Case Study School Standards

Enough work has been accomplished during the preceding exercises to apply the readers' concepts of principal evaluation to the case study. Remember that the case study school is privately owned by the principal's corporation.

[Note: for reader reference, the data about the case study principal and his school has been gathered under the heading "THE DATA LIST" and appears later in this chapter. THE DATA LIST is also reproduced in Appendix A.]

THE DATA LIST contains some items that describe what the case study school is expected to accomplish. This information is stated in the items numbered 13, 14, and 16. Readers should use the list they constructed in PE Task 1 (standards for a good school) and compare their standards with THE DATA LIST items that describe the standards for the case study school.

THE DATA LIST is organized as follows:

ITEMS	DESCRIBE
1 - 11	The school's physical qualities
12 - 28	Goals and program
29 - 36	Students and achievement
37 - 46	Staff
47 - 53	Finance
54 - 57.6	Community
58 - 70	Principal

DO PE TASK 7 NOW

Readers should compare their own lists of school standards (developed in PE Task 1) with the list of standards for the case study school in items 1 through 28 on THE DATA LIST. Items 13 and 14 state specifically what the case study school is expected to accomplish. Readers are encouraged to make written comments about any similarities and differences that they observe between the case study school standards and their own.

THE DATA LIST

School Description:

1. Name: The International School
2. Location: Somewhere in North America
3. Grades: Kindergarten Through Grade Eight
4. Enrollment: Two Hundred Students
5. Staff:
   (a) Eleven Regular Classroom Teachers
   (b) One Reading Specialist
   (c) One Resource Teacher
   (d) One Assistant Principal
   (e) One Principal/Chief Administrator
   (f) Two Secretaries
   (g) Eight Parent Volunteer Classroom Aids

   (Class size/staff size equals the average of similar schools.)
6. The school was built to serve children of families associated with an international water reclamation project.
7. The school operates under contract to a private corporation.
8. The principal is a major shareholder of the corporation.
9. The school is seven years old.
10. Most students stay two years, a few stay three years, and only two or three students stay four years, none longer.
11. Fifty percent of the students are American, the others are from more than a dozen nations (most come from European and Middle Eastern countries).
12. Parents are responsible for student transportation.
13. The contract requires a mainstream U.S. public school program for all students.

14. Students are expected to make their normal gains in performance and achievement while attending the school.
15. The school goals are understood and accepted by the staff and community.
16. The school program emphasizes basic skills and academics.
17. Art, music, and physical education instruction are conducted by the regular classroom teachers.
18. No shop, homemaking, typing or similar courses exist.
19. No standardized testing program is in place.
20. Student progress is assessed by teacher and principal observation in all curriculum areas.
21. The principal has agreed to use standardized tests of basic skills, in the future, and only with the American students.
22. The school has a twenty station computer lab.
23. Computer software is acquired from the public domain at little or no cost.
24. The third and fifth grade teachers use the computer lab according to their own interests.
25. No current plan exists to integrate the computer lab into the regular program.
26. The school needs playground and physical education equipment.
27. The school has adequate instructional supplies and materials.
28. Staff members conduct some after-school programs for students.
29. The school atmosphere reflects high levels of cooperation at both the student and staff levels.
30. Students appear to be above grade in their basic language and math skills, and in most academic courses.
31. Student achievement in science (grades seven and eight) appears to be below school standards.

32. No conflict between students of any age group is apparent.

33. The school has not had a serious student or staff member accident.

34. Minor student accidents (bumps and bruises) are at a minimal level.

35. Students appear to be working hard at their studies.

36. All students are capable of working in a regular school program.

37. Staff members appear to be working hard at their jobs.

38. Staff members are provided annual in-service education.

39. All school personnel act friendly toward each other and towards visitors.

40. An unqualified teacher teaches upper grade science.

41. Staff members appear to respect the principal.

42. Staff members do not take their complaints to the principal.

43. Some staff members complain privately about a work overload.

44. Forty-seven percent of the professional staff, including the principal, are members of the same small religious sect.

45. An acknowledged incompetent teacher was allowed to remain in the classroom for an entire school year without being re-assigned or dismissed.

46. Recruiting teachers for the school is difficult.

47. The principal has expensive computer and television equipment in his office for his own use.

48. The principal reports a small contingency reserve.

49. Tuition costs are at the ninetieth percentile of similar contract schools.

50. Tuition is paid by each parent's employer.

51. No employer has complained about tuition rates or refused or delayed payment.

52. The principal's residence is supported out of school funds in accordance with the school contract.

53. The principal reports that he has saved the school thousands of operating dollars because of his frugality.

Community Description:

54. The community is composed of water specialists and their families, including scientists, technicians, and laborers.

55. The great majority of parents are openly supportive of the school although they do want:

    55.1 A regular standardized testing program for American students

    55.2 An advisory group to review the school budget

56. The principal's home is one of the two best houses in the community.

57. A small group of parents have formally complained about:

    57.1 Religious imbalance of the staff

    57.2 An unqualified upper grade science teacher

    57.3 Inadequate PE equipment

    57.4 Inadequate after school programs for students

    57.5 Failure to dismiss an incompetent teacher mid-year due to poor budgeting for contingencies (such as hiring a replacement)

    57.6 Excessive funds used to support the principal's residence

Principal Description:

58. Credentialed English teacher and school administrator

59. "Thoreau-like" personality (self-existing), limited social skills

60. Considered unapproachable by staff

61. Regards himself as the local expert on school priorities

62. Has no close friends
63. Hard worker
64. Poor personnel recruiting skills (relies on staff members to recruit their friends)
65. Careful of money to the point of being penurious
66. Devotee of Mastery Learning
67. Experienced in nonstandard and overseas school operation and management
68. Asks for advice from those he respects, does not want unsolicited advice
69. Strong dislike for criticism, reduces school complaints to personality defects in the critic
70. Justifies his actions as being appropriate to his contract

PE Task 8: Selecting Data for Use in Making the Case Study Evaluation

The next step is to go over the entire DATA LIST and to identify all the items the reader considers relevant to and important for making an evaluation of the principal in the case study school.

[Note: **Readers may want to reread Chapter Two and underline those parts of the case study they want to utilize in making the evaluation before going back through THE DATA LIST.**]

Every item on the list should fall into one of three possible topic areas:

(a) examples of good school standards;

(b) examples of principal accountability; or

(c) examples of other categories (some of which may be similar to those listed by readers during PE Task 3).

DO PE TASK 8 NOW

Decide to which of the topic areas each item on THE DATA LIST belongs. Mark each item (including sub-numbers) with an appropriate "a", "b" or "c" category indicator.

[Suggestion: write the identifying numbers for items selected in category "b" in a separate location, preferably a sheet of paper, because the reader will be asked to compare those selected items later on with two other case study principal's evaluations, and having such a list will make it easier to conduct the comparisons.]

PE Task 9: Ranking the Data in Terms of Its Importance

The list has eighty-six items (which are too much to keep in mind). Re-reading Chapter Two can help to put the data in a context, but even doing that has its limits. No matter how good their immediate recall capabilities, readers will have to do some sorting and prioritizing to make the data useful for making an evaluation.

DO PE TASK 9 NOW

Begin the sorting and prioritizing process by marking each item selected for evaluating the principal with a "1" (most important), "2" (average importance), or "3" (less important). Readers should simply ignore those items that have no bearing on their evaluations.

Having identified all the items on THE DATA LIST to be used in the evaluation and having finished sorting and prioritizing the items, the reader may see the need for additional information that was not on the list. For purposes of this exercise, assume it does not exist or is neutral, neither positive enough nor negative enough to change the outcome of the final evaluation.

PE Task 10: Grouping the Data According to Each Criterion

DO TASK 10 NOW

Using the evaluation criteria developed during PE Task 3, write out each DATA LIST item number, rated "1," "2" or "3," under the readers' appropriate criterion headings. Write the items rated "1" before those rated "2" and so forth, thereby keeping the highest priority items at the top of each cluster. In some instances an item may be deemed to belong under more than a single criterion. If this happens, list such items under each appropriate heading.

PE Task 11: Comparing the Data with the Criteria and Making Judgments

Now that the data is properly prioritized and grouped, it is time to judge the items that will be of greatest importance in setting up the Principal Evaluation System Document for evaluating the case study principal. Naturally, some data is more important than others, just as some standards are more important than others. Even some important data is of greater significance than other important data. Therefore, the reader is encouraged to select no more than a dozen highest priority items. Selecting at least a dozen items focuses the evaluation and more clearly pinpoints the specifics for which the evaluator will hold the principal accountable. The ensuing evaluation will then deal with significant matters, either positive or negative (or both) and thereby put minor (and in some instances, trivial) concerns into proper perspective. Later on, the identification of the highest priority items will also tell something about the reader's evaluation philosophy.

This final revised list constitutes a list of "findings" that will be referred to in the final written evaluation document.

Remember that the final evaluation document is for someone else, "The Third Party," to read. The evaluation is a comparison between the standards and the findings made by using criteria which indicate how well the standards have been met.

DO PE TASK 11 NOW

Readers should write a series of judgment statements regarding how well the case study principal is carrying out his job. A separate judgment statement should be written for each criteria named during PE Task 3. Each judgment statement should include a reference to the standard of accountability the principal should have met and the "findings" (made in PE Task 10) which led to the judgment.

The material produced during this step in the evaluation process constitutes the "rough notes" that an evaluator uses in preparing the final written evaluation document. Such notes are written to the writer (the evaluator), to serve his or her own recollections and make sure that nothing has been forgotten. Should an evaluator face a "Third Party" to explain these judgments, the rough notes prepared at this step would be handy reminders describing exactly how the evaluator went about preparing the final written evaluation document.

PE Task 12: Preparing the Final Written Evaluation Document

Formal evaluation systems should always specify the name(s) and job title(s) of the person (people) who will evaluate the principal. In this exercise the reader is the evaluator. In some school systems principals are formally evaluated by more than one person; for example, curriculum functions may be evaluated by one person and business functions evaluated by another.

Written evaluations take whatever form the system chooses. The first part of a formal evaluation document typically has the usual dates and names. The document should contain a statement of findings and judgments for each evaluation criterion based on the rough notes produced in PE Task 11. The document should report how well the principal's school is meeting the adopted school system standards. The document should recommend subsequent actions to affect the principal or state what actions were taken and by whom.

The following procedure is recommended: under each criterion heading write a statement of what was found and how the findings compare with the criteria the reader developed during PE Task 3. Then write individual statements that describe how well the school is meeting each standard. Again, the reader is to use the standards written in PE Task 1. Does the data warrant a commendation? If so, commend the principal. Should the principal be excused for not meeting any standard? Then say so, and give the reason. "I don't think anyone could do any better," and "He didn't measure up on this, but it's a minor concern" are two acceptable reasons.

If the description of findings and how well a standard was met do not automatically convey what is required for the principal to meet the standard, then include a statement of what is required to meet the standard.

DO PE TASK 12 NOW

Readers are not asked to write a complete final evaluation document for the case study principal. They have completed enough work to know how they would proceed with such a task if it were given to them. However, readers should write out a recommendation for action to be taken with the case study principal according to one of the five options that were presented:

1. Nothing at all
2. A bonus for operating a superior school
3. A censure for poor performance in certain areas which could result in withholding some funding
4. Allow the school to continue operation only with a change of administrator
5. Termination of the schools' operation contract

Moving on to Chapters Four and Five

The next two chapters present the rationales and descriptions of two competing approaches to principal evaluation:

The first approach is a "Results-Based" evaluation. "Results-Based" evaluators have little or no concern for processes, per se; they are interested in school outcomes.

The second approach is a "Performance-Based" evaluation. "Performance-Based" evaluators focus their personnel evaluations on how well employees follow performance standards accepted and adopted within the professional community.

When these two chapters are completed, the readers will compare the PE Tasks just completed with those presented in the examples in Chapters 4 and 5. The comparison will help to point out the reader's philosophy for making evaluations of principals.

4

Results-Based Principal Evaluation

This chapter presents a discussion of the "results-based" principal evaluation system. The advocate for this approach is called Mr. Results. He believes that the measurement of what the school accomplishes, its outcomes, is the only reasonable basis for evaluating school principals. Mr. Results isn't searching for a philosophy for making principal evaluations because he has already found one. He expects everyone to agree with his position. However, not everyone does agree.

Chapter Five presents a similar discussion of another approach to principal evaluation: "performance-based" principal evaluation. Its advocate is Mr. Performance. Mr. Performance will tell readers about his philosophy in the next chapter. For now, readers need only recognize that the assumptions underlying the two approaches to principal evaluation, results-based and performance-based, are opposed to one another.

Mr. Results and Mr. Performance are neither heroes nor villains. Both are humanitarians; both are concerned with the quality of cognitive and affective learnings in schools; and both recognize the need for physical education as well as the need for educating the mind. They share an equal concern for good education, and each recognizes that school principals are the key to school improvement. Mr. Results and Mr. Performance agree with each other on definitions of good schools, and they agree on the details of what constitutes good education. However, they disagree on the basis for evaluating school principals.

Both advocates follow the same format for their presentations: both Mr. Results and Mr. Performance profess to have determined "the only way" to carry out the principal evaluation process.

The openings of both Chapters Four and Five discuss one or the other advocate's rationale, his assumptions about evaluating principals and the fairness of his position. Each discussion is followed by an evaluation of the case study principal, Mr. Swenson. Mr. Results evaluates Mr. Swenson from his results-based point of view, and Mr. Performance evaluates Mr. Swenson from his performance-based viewpoint.

The discussions and the sample evaluations given by Mr. Results and Mr. Performance will serve to explore their two approaches to evaluating principals, show the processes followed by each, present the bases for their respective judgments, and compare the contents of their final written evaluation documents.

The presentations in this chapter and the next may raise questions for readers about topics that neither Mr. Results nor Mr. Performance raise. Should this happen and readers have questions not answered, they are urged to remember that the book's intention is for readers to develop their own individual systems for principal evaluation, according to their own values; not merely to adopt values from someone else. If at any point readers feel they have found flaws or gaps in either advocacy, results-based or performance-based, they should note, avoid, or compensate for these flaws in their own principal evaluation systems.

PART 1—EVALUATING THE RESULTS

The Only Rational Basis for Evaluating a Principal

In the corporate business world, the criteria for success are little more than a short list of "bottom line" results. The fundamental criteria are profits and productivity. Since the Seventies, a few new items have been added: ecological impacts and affirmative action results are two common examples. Executives are held accountable for corporate results, while subordinate managers are accountable for the results from their respective divisions, plants, and sections.

- Receipts exceeded expenses.
- The contract was signed.
- The affirmative action goals were met.
- The E.P.A. standards were met.
- No excuses, please. Just the bottom line.

Every bottom line is a composite result, actually the result of several bottom lines, each of which must be achieved in order to generate the final result, the final "bottom line."

Consider the following sequence:

The company product must work at each stage of production if it is to work as a finished item. Also, the product must be sold, be delivered on time and must remain working. The sales contract must clarify responsibilities for buyer and seller, include provisions for yielding a profit and be signed by all parties. Each step involves workers and managers. The managers are assigned responsibilities and held accountable for the results. The managers' results are evaluated. If they are successful, they keep their jobs. If they are extremely successful, they get raises or promotions (even the keys to the executive washroom). If they are only somewhat successful, they may fall into an uncomfortable condition called "probation." If they are consistently unsuccessful, they are either "out of the company" or relegated to a position without real responsibilities, and their careers grind to a halt. This system has proven to be fair and rational, and is supported by tradition.

Public opinion demands parallels between the ways of business and the ways of public schools. Often, however, there is no basis of comparison. As a result, some school administrators have skillfully assembled an ever-expanding list of "reasons" why they cannot be held accountable for the bottom line. Yet, this is a "bottom line" society. Why shouldn't all school administrators accept responsibility for the schools they manage? Superintendents are responsible for the schools under their jurisdiction, and individual school principals are responsible for their schools. Their own literature, their own research, suggest that an individual school's success results from the competency of its building principal. Doesn't the logic of reality demand that all principals should be held accountable for their schools in the same way that plant managers in the economy's private sector are held accountable?

Is this too simplistic? Is it too harsh? Many experienced school administrators believe that quota-evaluation is appropriate for sales and assembly line managers but not for those whose work cannot be measured in units such as dollars or ball bearings.

Are test scores and attendance records as clearly definable as dollars or ball bearings? Does it matter that the units are different? The public, the media, parents, politicians and educators are already evaluating schools. They use an assortment of measurement devices such as test scores and earned honors (which can be regarded as "results"), and those measures are the school outcomes in which people are interested.

Active participants in the school system and outside observers alike are confused about how well their schools are doing when their school systems have not specified the school outcomes toward which they are working. The confusion is reduced in school systems that specify which measures will be used to judge the sufficiency of their schools.

Remember Parkinson's Law? "Sufficient work will be created to fill the available time." Parkinson wrote a serious book about serious economic problems, and people laughed.

They did not laugh at "him." They laughed at their own absurdities that he had identified.

He was concerned about organizational problems that get in the way of achieving organizational goals. The heart of his remarkable law was his observation that workers tend to focus on how they are doing the job, rather than on what their work is supposed to produce. Isn't this an excellent description of what schools do? Isn't it what they have always done?

Yet, the argument is to measure school excellence based on results. Now, whose job is it to see that a school produces results? If it is not the principal's job, who is left? Without principal accountability, is there any hope of meeting the students', the parents' and the public's expectations for their schools?

A results-based evaluation system puts a proper focus on the evaluation process for both the people being evaluated and for the evaluators making the judgments about them, because both evaluatee and evaluator know that it is results that count.

Managers should not be on trial; they are not defendants. What the organization accomplishes should be evaluated, and the manager should be held accountable for those accomplishments that pertain to his area of responsibility. The evaluator should judge what the organization produces, not how the manager behaves.

Define Your Principal's Accountability

Evaluators should ask themselves this question: "Are the principals in my school system managers (whose duties include supervision), or are they just supervisors?" "Do the principals direct and carry on—manage—school operations such as planning the school's overall operation, allocating funds, selecting and assigning staff, and establishing programs; or do they simply direct their subordinates' work according to a higher authority's plan?" (Remember the answers and the reasons for saying so.) Evaluators and principals alike should know how much initiative the principals can exercise in their own schools.

Principals are managers if they have a defined freedom of action, if they use their own initiative, and if they are held fully accountable for the schools under their jurisdiction. Managers seek advice often, permission seldom.

If the principal is not a manager, and consequently not accountable for his or her school, who is? Think seriously about this question and there is only one answer: the responsible person is whoever lets the principal off the hook.

The accountability of managers is made obvious by the specifics in their evaluations which will judge them as proactive or reactive.

Many school system administrators already use "recognition letters" and "warning letters" in their principal evaluation programs. They give promotions and demotions. A results-based principal evaluation system establishes a highly defensible basis for any personnel action to be taken "for" or "against" a principal, because the basis for such judgments (the "results") are clearly identifiable when the desired outcomes are specified before the principal's work begins.

A distinct advantage of a results-based system is that the data which forms the basis of the evaluation is much less ambiguous than a description of how someone behaved.

Evaluators may forgive bad results; they may ignore good results—those choices are left to evaluators. The ultimate integrity of all evaluation systems depends on how well the evaluators do their jobs, and results-based evaluation systems reveal the quality of evaluators' work more readily than any other system approach because the data used is less ambiguous than the data used with other evaluation methods. The data used in a results-based evaluation system reveals school outcomes which are the proper points-of-focus for creating good schools.

Focus on Good Results

The focus of a principal's evaluation should be on the results his leadership has produced. A skilled principal will turn a bad school into a good one. Repeated examples exist of dynamic, forceful, and autocratic men and women changing disinterested non-focused slum schools into thriving educational establishments inundated with pride and dedication. Repeated examples exist of quiet, thoughtful, and democratic men and women doing the same thing. And, there are schools that at one time had been supported by community and staff, where the curriculum was challenging, and children had been eager and successful learners, but which were later turned into cesspools of intrigue, distrust, and distraction by principals (perhaps successful in other settings) who could not manage an established successful school. Since both situations are demonstrably true, why should school systems focus on the qualities of the principal when society must focus on the results the principal produces. Admittedly, there are minimal qualities which should be characteristic of every principal. The minimal qualities are supposed to be discerned before a principal is hired. Individual track records reveal the character of candidates for principal, such as hard working, ethical, knowledgeable about curriculum and management procedures, and able to work with others. Principal evaluation occurs after the position is filled and results are what the principal is supposed to produce.

Is there actually such a thing as a good principal in a bad school? Certainly there are principals who are good people who are in bad schools, but that doesn't mean that a good person is also a good principal. There are principals in low achieving, disorderly schools who appear to act in all the prescribed ways, but the students in the school do not improve. It is not the responsibility of the principal to behave as a theoretically "good" principal behaves. It is the responsibility of the principal to do whatever is necessary to produce a safe and orderly school where student achievement improves.

The Community and the Principal Expect Fair Treatment

Both parties to an employment contract expect fairness and justice. Likewise, the principal's evaluation system must assure these. Principals cannot work effectively when subjected to threats of dismissal that result from momentary whims that occur to an employer, and employers should not be forced to bear with principals who ignore the school system's goals and priorities. The principal must be respected and so must the public. Those served by the principal evaluation system must believe that the system is fair, or it will fail.

Fairness for the Principal

Many factors are beyond a principal's control. Inequities exist between schools and uncertainties exist within schools. Considerable ambiguity is connected with the job of being principal. Knowing this, can we still hold principals accountable for results? Consider this: All managers (in factories, banks, conglomerates, schools, wherever) work in an ambiguous environment; in fact, all professionals work in an ambiguous environment. Ambiguity is a condition administrators must learn to deal with because it will always show up one time or another. It is fair to hold managers in other fields accountable for their results. Why, then, is it not fair to treat school principals in the same way?

Logic requires some persuasive data to justify excluding school managers from the same kind of accountability as other managers. The purpose of all personnel evaluation systems is to enforce some kind of accountability. Results-based evaluation systems for school principals require that principals be given the same freedom of action as other managers, and that, given the same degrees of freedom as other managers, school principals may be fairly held accountable for results. Of course, no one has complete freedom of action: all managers, however powerful, must operate within some constraints.

Consideration must be given to the person being evaluated. An evaluation system that is explicit in its expectations and gives assurances of due process meets the basic principles of fairness and social justice demanded by fair-minded people. The question, again, "What is fair for the principals who are expected to create good schools?"

First, it is fair that the principal should have prior knowledge of the school characteristics (or standards) that his leadership is expected to achieve.

Second, it is fair that clearly defined information about the expected characteristics should be available to the principal.

Third, it is fair that after the evaluation procedure has transpired, the principal should be advised that a discrepancy between school conditions and school expectations has been observed and noted by the evaluator. (Feedback).

Fourth, it is fair that the principal should be provided with a reasonable amount of time in which to correct any deficiencies.

Fifth, it is fair that the principal should be provided with assistance in efforts to correct any deficiencies.

Sixth, it is fair that excellent principals should be rewarded (preferably in pre-established ways), and persistently poor principals should be removed from their positions (after corrective efforts have failed).

Principals deserve these assurances.

Fairness for the Public

It is fair that appropriate schools reflect the will of the public, because the public supports the existence of the schools and suffers most when schools fail.

People created the school system. They support employment of school personnel to implement a system that will serve their purposes. Schools are not created, and run, to serve the school employees. Schools are not even created to serve the demands of students. Schools are there to serve what the public wants. Determining school standards, goals and purposes, and setting standards for student behavior are public responsibilities. The public deserves assurance that its purposes and requirements are continuously and diligently addressed. Anything less is unfair.

A Summary of the Rationale for a Results-Based System

1. The public deserves excellent schools.
2. The principal is supposed to be qualified to administer a school, has been given the responsibility to do so, and is accountable for the nature of the stewardship.
3. The expectations regarding the conditions to be found in particular schools and particular school systems must be stated and made clear to the principal.
4. Credible information about the school, its personnel and its students must be gathered. The information should relate to pre-established criteria.
5. The expectations stated and the information gathered must be rationally analyzed, compared, and reported, after which a determination is to be made about the extent to which there are (or are not) discrepancies.
6. These judgments must be shared with the principal at a suitable time, and he must be given a reasonable amount of time to institute correction.
7. The principal will be given reasonable help, advice, and encouragement.
8. Excellence in principal performance will be rewarded, whereas insufficiency or a lack of success will not be tolerated.

[This concludes Mr. Results' rationale for using a results-based evaluation system.]

PART 2—THE PROCESS

Carrying out a Results-Based Principal Evaluation System

The essence of any good system is to make the complex manageable; to distinguish "useful" data from trivial data. The "important" is ranked above the less important. Data which is "required" are extracted from total data and made available for use in carrying out the evaluation.

Personnel evaluation generates a deluge of data. Evaluators must organize it into a sensible form, arranged so they can look at the data in small clusters that have some common meaning. Every personnel evaluation system establishes categories for grouping data so that everything is not looked at in the same instant. The purpose of categories is to offer some reassurance that everything that is judged does receive due consideration, and that irrelevant information can safely be cast aside. A results-based evaluation system defines relevant data as being the only data that pertains; all else is not useful and is irrelevant.

Five General Criteria for Data, Data Collection and Making Judgments in a Results-Based Principal Evaluation System

Five conditions exist in all "good" schools:

1. The school is safe for students, staff and visitors.
2. The school programs get positive, beneficial results.
3. School systems and activities in the school have recognized and accepted purposes.
4. The people are at work (school personnel, and students).
5. The principal is a district statesman.

Each of these five conditions will be discussed in some detail. (But, why not one criterion? Or, why not six, seven or fifteen criteria?) Actually, there is no absolute, all inclusive magic number of criteria. Nevertheless, Mr. Results finds these five conditions to be practical, easily understood, comprehensive and consistent with his philosophy of looking at results. He does not insist that these are the only, and, perhaps, not even the best criteria, but they work for him.

Think back to the case study school in Chapter Two. Wasn't that unusual little school succeeding, not completely, but in most ways? First, it is a very safe school, physically and psychologically. Second, the school gets positive results. It meets the general emotional and academic needs of students, as witnessed by the high level of support from the vast majority of parents. Third, the school's primary educational purpose is to serve students for a year or two before they return home, and both the students and their parents expect their student academic standing to be equal to or above their stay-at-home peers. The school does all this. Fourth, the school is obviously a cooperative working place where people work hard. Staff members communicate openly, share, and help one another. The parents volunteer their time and talents.

Fifth, the principal is clearly the spokesman for the company that owns and operates the school. It is a private school, owned and operated by a corporation in which the school principal is also a key stockholder. He is unorthodox. His methods are kindly but direct. He makes it clear that the power to make decisions is his; advice is useful, sometimes desired, but authority is not shared. As is, he wouldn't last very long—perhaps a week—in many American public school systems. He isn't diplomatic; whether he needs to be is subject to individual judgment.

One purpose for using a contrived example is that it focuses our attention on a single school in its own context. We also hold some common concerns for all schools. For example, we want all students to grow up and become acceptable adults. While in school they should be physically and emotionally cared for, and they should acquire the necessary knowledge and skills to carry on the culture. Yet, every school operates within its own special context, taking into account what kind of school it is, as well as the requirements of the state, region, and community in which it exists.

The five general criteria listed above apply to all schools, reflecting people's concerns with schools in general, and the five criteria will serve as a basis for judging schools everywhere.

Getting Results

Americans are competitive, "results-oriented" people. But, there are no profit-and-loss statements to use to measure nonprofit schools. So, "results" from its schools are difficult to evaluate. Yet, measurable results are needed by the general public to maintain a sense of purpose and confidence to maintain public support for the institution.

Discussions, debates, arguments, and rumors rage in, around, and about every school. These are sometimes referred to as "the informal communications network." However, not all rumors are bad, not all debates are fair, and not all discussions are rational. The result of all these various communications is the "message" that gives each school its "reputation." How ironic it is that rumor is the most common means of knowing that a school is good. Good schools attend to this by building a body of evidence supporting their accomplishments. The evidence is circulated widely and discussed often.

What kind of evidence do schools use? Many things, including:

- statistics
- scores
- reports
- awards
- budgets
- testimonials

and whatever else the community accepts as valid measures of accomplishment.

Evidence and events are the substance behind the informal communication network (the rumor mill) that gives the school its real reputation. In the final analysis, nothing is more important to the long term well-being of a school than having a positive image.

Safety

Few people name "safety" as a first concern for a good school, probably only those who have experienced a problem would do so. Safety is an unspoken "given" in the operation of a good school.

Hazards often appear to be obvious, but safety hazards typically develop when routine procedures and general supervision requirements are ignored.

The following considerations are basic for school safety standards.

1. Completed maintenance requests result in fewer human hazards and longer-lasting buildings.

2. Routine inspections of food services, water supply, cleanliness and equipment safety provide a safer environment.

3. Student safety includes protection from serious peer abuse. (Most thugs start out as playground bullies, stealing lunch money and beating up the defenseless. Certain pre-adolescent girls are known for tormenting other children for no other reason than the sport of it.)

4. There are (or have been) instances of physical beatings and sexual abuse of students by teachers and other staff members in school. The subtle use of racial, ethnic or religious discrimination is more difficult to detect, but these intolerable behaviors sometimes do occur.

5. The child with self-destructive tendencies or pathetic social skills needs help. Such cases may be few, but they exist in virtually every school.

6. The community surrounding the school may have threatening elements: the junior high that becomes a battle ground for youths from the neighboring high school, or the presence of perverted adults wanting access to children.

Each of these items is a safety problem. But, is any school safe in the sense that it is free from all possible hazards? No, but the potential hazards can be dramatically reduced. It is undoubtedly true that most schools are mainly safe, even if they have a particular safety problem.

The annual Gallup Education Poll consistently lists student physical well-being as the top concern of school parents. "Discipline" also has topped the list for many years. In 1987

"Drug Abuse" was rated the number one concern and "Discipline" became number two. Safety and discipline are not identical, but a well-disciplined school is a characteristic of a safe school, and a safe school (in the fullest sense of the word "safe") is recognized as a well-disciplined school.

Purpose/Goals

The purpose for which the school in the case study exists is clear. It is to serve students from various countries for a year or two before they return to their regular home schools. It is a small school with a somewhat homogeneous population, which is common for schools constructed to serve special groups of students. Specialty schools address narrower aims than most public schools.

The time was, in the not too distant past, when the public schools had narrower purposes than today. Now, the public school goal is quite literally to "educate everyone." As a result, the job is more complex, and the goals and objectives have expanded. The expansion is both a cause for celebrating our confidence in education, and a source of confusion over our new directions. Confusion of purpose is as unsettling to the school atmosphere as unstable air masses are to an airplane.

Good schools state their goals and objectives clearly so that they will be understood and supported by their communities, staffs and students. The standards are constantly reinforced, not left as mere words on paper. General goal statements are handed down from a higher authority, and individual schools refine the broad aims to match the needs and behaviors of their students. Each teacher, each professional staff member in a good school, has his or her own professional objectives, planned activities and assessment procedures for implementing the school goals.

A Cooperative Working Environment

The most obvious quality observed in a good school is the work activity of the people in the school. Teachers are teaching, students are studying and the other personnel are active at their jos as well. Even the youngster slumped in an office chair, dejectedly waiting to see the principal, is involved in the process of education. (He is where he belongs at the moment, doing what he should be doing at the moment.) It is difficult, nearly impossible, to remain anonymous on a good school campus, where both aimless and extraordinary behavior are noticed and called into question.

The untutored observer on a good school's campus is apt to see efficient and effective work in the same way some people watch professional athletes. Remarkable plays seem routine to those who know little of the game. Teamwork and "assists" are taken for granted. It is often easier to describe the "errors." It's easy to spot such problems as:

1. Workers (staff and students) constantly asking for help, not knowing how or what to do.
2. Work (classroom and otherwise) is capriciously interrupted by "messages," and the like.
3. The prominence of idle talk, not job related.
4. The presence of sloppy, dirty work spaces.
5. An attitude of unfriendliness.
6. The sight of people not working.
7. Workers ignoring details, not following posted directions.
8. The refusal of people to give assistance when asked.

In a positive school environment, an observer sees people knowing what to do and how to do it, and doing it well. Furthermore, a spirit of cooperation emanates from all the parties, paid employees and volunteers alike. The work of a school is teaching and learning. The support activities of everyone else, from the office staff to the custodians, reflect this priority.

Hard work and cooperation were major strong qualities of the case study school. That dedication was deeply appreciated by the parents. The school was rewarded for hard work by a high level of community support, and in spite of some concerns by many people (and serious concerns expressed by a few), most of the parents had pride in the school. Active and cooperative parent participation is often associated with good schools.

Principals as School System Statesmen

Principals are agents for their employers. Their contracts are predicated on a presumption that they are of good character, that they are moral and ethical. Public school principals speak for their school systems; they speak for their superintendents; they are officials in an organization larger than their individual schools. Their relationships to their employers are not the same as the relationships between other employees and employers; professional loyalty is a part of their agreement to work as administrators. The consequences of their conduct can be public credibility and support for their school systems, or the results can be disruption and problems. Therefore, any principal who lies, cheats, or steals is subject to dismissal.

The evaluator of a principal's performance shouldn't have to make continuous assessments within this category (the principal's role as statesmen), unless some evidence emerges to call it into question. Then the evaluator is obligated to trace it down and verify whether or not the source and evidence are accurate.

Assessing School Quality

What is the line that separates a good school from a mediocre or bad school? There may be a finite answer, but usually the answer is subjective. It depends on the varied judgments of various people.

One historical influence on judging school quality is based on national reports on the schools. National school reports have focused on the "Deficiencies in Schools." Virtually no national report extols school accomplishments. Yet, national polls, such as the Gallup Poll, consistently show that parents appreciate their children's teachers. The most recent Gallup polls show that those closest to the schools have the best opinions of the schools. (But, these are, of course, opinions, not objective measurements.)

Education is not a science. It is a practitioner's "art" that tries to form its theories from both scientific findings and the collective experience of practitioners in the field. In these respects it resembles the practice of medicine. No one knows how learning occurs, and no one knows why the heart beats. Not knowing either of these things does not close schools, or discontinue heart surgery, but it points up an interesting comparison between physicians and educators: both are "practitioners of an art," and not scientists. As such, they deserve to be judged in terms of the realities of their fields, not according to hypothetical and futuristic fantasy. (Admittedly, doctors get closer to becoming scientists than educators. Education is a "mixed bag" filled with some knowledge and a lot of opinion. The greatest amount of what is known about education comes from a thousand years of practice. The rest of what we know about the process of education comes from behavioral science theories.)

It is known that some schools make greater progress than others. Some schools have better achievement records and their students show significant progress. Evidence of progress has come to be the criteria for labeling a school an "effective school." The five evaluation categories described in this chapter are consistent with the findings of "effective schools" studies conducted in California, New York, Massachusetts and other states. From a school management point of view, the most significant single finding of these studies was the critical role of the principal in causing a school to become an "effective school."

PART 3—EXAMINING THE CASE STUDY DATA FOR A RESULTS-BASED EVALUATION

[NOTE: Mr. Results now applies his concept of a "Results-Based" evaluation system to the case study of Principal Swenson. In preparation, Mr. Results first reviewed the case study material and identified all the data that he considered to be relevant to his evaluation. Readers may agree or disagree with his specific choices. By comparing their lists with his, they should be able to tell by the number of common choices whether or not they are in fundamental agreement with his approach, the "results-based" approach, to principal evaluation.]

The Base Line Evaluation—Advocate's Report

This is a "Base Line" evaluation (of Mr. John Swenson and his International School), meaning it is the first evaluation on record, and no previous evaluation exists for comparative purposes.

All data was collected by the evaluator during a three-day on-site visit to the school. A complete transcript of the record of that visit is attached. The data is a collection of direct observations and oral reports to the evaluator.

From the evaluator's case study data, THE DATA LIST, Mr. Results would identify four items as indicators of expected school standards. The items are considered to constitute the standards or are related to establishing the standards for judging the school. (Readers should note that the number alongside each item corresponds to the same item number on the case study DATA LIST.) When readers complete reading Mr. Results' evaluation document, they will see how he has used these items as standards for forming his judgments:

13. The contract requires a mainstream U.S. public school program for all students.

14. Students are expected to make their normal gain in performance and achievement while attending the school.

36. All students are capable of working in a regular school program.

52. The principal's residence is supported out of school funds in accordance with the school contract.

Mr. Results identified the following items as school outcomes that were considered useful in making a results-based evaluation. Items marked with a double asterisk (**) were considered most important. Items marked with a single asterisk (*) were considered of secondary importance. The unmarked items on Mr. Results' outcomes list would be considered appropriate to a results-based evaluation, but not especially meaningful in this evaluation. Mr. Results would believe that the principal is accountable for the following outcomes:

15.** The school goals are understood and accepted by the staff and community.

16.* The school program emphasizes basic skills and academics.

18.** No shop, homemaking, typing or similar courses exist.

19.* No standardized testing program is in place.

21. The principal has agreed to use standardized tests of basic skills in the future, and only with the American students.

22. The school has a twenty station computer lab.

24. The third and fifth grade teachers use the computer lab according to their own interests.

25.* No current plan exists to integrate the computer lab into the regular program.

26.** The school needs playground and physical education equipment.

27.* The school has adequate instructional supplies and materials.

28. Staff members conduct some after-school programs for students.

29.** The school atmosphere reflects high levels of cooperation at both the student and staff levels.

30.** Students appear to be above grade in their basic language and math skills, and in most academic courses.

31.** Student achievement in science (grades seven and eight) appears to be below school standards.

32.** No conflict between students of any age group is apparent.

33.** The school has not had a serious student or staff member accident.

34.* Minor student accidents (bumps and bruises) are at a minimal level.

35.** Students appear to be working hard at their studies.

37.** Staff members appear to be working hard at their jobs.

39.* All school personnel act friendly toward each other and towards visitors.

44.** Forty-seven percent of the professional staff, including the principal, are members of the same small religious sect.

45. An acknowledged incompetent teacher was allowed to remain in the classroom for an entire school year without being re-assigned or dismissed.

47. The principal has expensive computer and television equipment in his office for his own use.

48. The principal reports a small contingency reserve.

50.* Tuition is paid by each parent's employer.

51.* No employer has complained about tuition rates or refused or delayed payment.

53. The principal reports that he has saved the school thousands of operating dollars because of his frugality.

55.** The great majority of parents are openly supportive of the school although they do want:

55.1* A regular standardized testing program for American students

55.2 An advisory group to review the school budget

56. The principal's home is one of the two best houses in the community.

57. A small group of parents have formally complained about:

57.1* Religious imbalance of the staff

57.2* An unqualified upper grade science teacher

57.3* Inadequate Pysical Education equipment

57.4 Inadequate after school programs for students

57.5 Failure to dismiss an incompetent teacher mid-year due to poor budgeting for contingencies (such as hiring a replacement)

57.6 Excessive funds used to support the principal's residence

The data was reviewed and ranked (most important, somewhat important, least important, and some was ignored). Mr. Results' marks by the items reflect his judgment of each items' importance to the evaluation he is conducting.

As a further refinement, he clusters the items he selected according to the five general criteria, GC1 - GC5, that he identified in his opening statement which described the "results-based" principal evaluation:

- GC1 = safety
- GC2 = results
- GC3 = goals and purpose
- GC4 = work
- GC5 = statesmanship

GC1. The school is safe:

32.** No conflict between students of any age group is apparent.

33.** The school has not had a serious student or staff member accident.

34.* Minor student accidents (bumps and bruises) are at a minimum.

GC2. The school programs and activities get positive results:

16.* The school program emphasizes basic skills and academics.

18.** No shop, homemaking, typing, or similar courses exist.

19.* No standardized testing program is in place.

26.** The school needs playground and physical education equipment.

30.** Students appear to be above grade in their basic language and math skills, and most academic courses.

31.** Student achievement in science (grades seven and eight) appears to be below school standards.

GC3. The school has recognized and accepted purposes:

15.** The school's goals are understood and accepted by the staff and the community.

18.** No shop, homemaking, typing or similar courses exist.

26.** The school needs playground and physical education equipment.

25.* No current plans exist to integrate the computer lab into the regular program.

51.* No employer has complained about tuition rates or refused or delayed payment.

GC4. The people are at work:

29.** The school atmosphere reflects high levels of cooperation at both the student and staff levels.

35.** Students appear to be working hard at their studies.

37.** Staff members appear to be working hard at their jobs.

39.* All school personnel act friendly toward each other and towards visitors.

GC5. The principal as a statesman:

44.** Forty-seven percent of the professional staff, including the principal, are members of the same small religious sect.

49.* Tuition costs are at the ninetieth percentile of similar contract schools.

27.* The school has adequate instructional supplies and materials.

School Supporters Want:

55.1* A regular standardized testing program for American students

School Critics' Complaints:

57.1* Religious imbalance of the staff

57.2* An unqualified upper grade science teacher

57.3* Inadequate physical education equipment

57.5* Failure to dismiss an incompetent teacher midyear due to poor budgeting for contingencies

The Written Evaluation

Bearing in mind all the evaluator has seen, heard, and concluded, he prepares Mr. Swenson's final principal evaluation document. The essential elements of his evaluation focus on the five conditions he believes exist in all "good" schools:

1. The school is safe for students, staff and visitors.
2. The school programs get positive, beneficial results.
3. All systems and activities in the school have recognized and accepted purposes.
4. The people are at work (school personnel and students).
5. The principal is a district statesman.

[NOTE: Such documents are official records typically kept in the individual employee's personnel files and are the property of the employer. The principal evaluation documents are prepared for a third party to review.

Whoever supervises (or employs) the evaluator is the most likely third party to review an evaluation. Looking beyond that, law cases that involve personnel and go to court place the evaluation in the court's hands. In this case study, the evaluator is a government consultant hired specifically for this purpose. The report will be sent to the evaluator's employer who has never seen the school or met Mr. Swenson. A copy will be given to the principal.]

Mr. Results' Written Evaluation

Dated this date
From: Mr. Results
To: Government Overseas Education Officer
Subject: Evaluation of John Swenson

Background Data:

Mr. Swenson is the principal and administrator in charge of the International School, located somewhere in North America. He has held this position for seven years.

The school serves the children of families in an international water project. There are no special education or handicapped students. The student body numbers 200 students. Attendance at this school usually lasts for two years, after which time students return to their home communities.

School Goals and Objectives:

The government contract with the school requires a mainstream U.S. public school program, kindergarten through grade eight. Students are expected to make normal achievement gains while attending this school.

Findings and Judgments:

1. **Safety**: The school has an outstanding safety record. The emotional climate for students is nurturant and supportive. There are no evident discipline problems. Mr. Swenson deserves commendation for superior results in this area.

2. **Results**: My professional judgment, based on direct observation, supports the conclusion that student achievement in basic skill courses, and most academic courses, is well above average. However, upper grade science

achievement is decidedly low (for this student population) and requires improvement.

Mr. Swenson is responsible for providing standardized test information to parents, students and staff, yet he has not provided a standardized testing program for his school. This omission is fundamentally important in that it interferes with judging the school's effectiveness. Parents, teachers, and students have a need, and a right, to be supplied with this data.

3. **Recognized and Accepted Purposes**: The basic skills and academic goals of the school are well understood, accepted, and supported by students, staff, and parents. The degree of common acceptance and support is exceptional. The private corporation and other nations which contribute to the school's operating budget have implied their support of the school's aims by prompt, regular payment of fees without any questions.

   Mr. Swenson has not fully met the expectations of the contract. He has failed to provide adequately for non-academic subjects (i.e., typing, computer literacy, computer programming) in the upper grade and physical education needs in all grades. A mainstream U.S. education requires attention to these student needs. Students are entitled to study in these subject areas. Mr. Swenson should insure that students achieve in these areas.

4. **People at Work**: The work behavior in the school is as good as I have ever seen, from the youngest students to the oldest, the staff, volunteers and visiting parents. People are cheerful, cooperative, and they have purpose. Mr. Swenson has produced excellent results in this area.

5. **Statesmanship**: Mr. Swenson enjoys a remarkably high level of community support. Although subject to occasional outbursts of criticism from a small group of parents, nevertheless he was strongly supported by the majority. He also seems to ignore the criticisms, with the result that some legitimate negative impressions have been created about the issues raised by the small group. These could become serious problems in the future.

Besides the eight locally hired teachers (all spouses of project employees), all other teaching and professional staff members which were recruited by Mr. Swenson belong to a single small religious sect (to which Mr. Swenson also belongs). This religious selectivity is unjustified. Parental concerns for possible religious indoctrination of their children is an untenable school outcome.

The community is of the impression that the school operates with a tight budget and that funds are limited. Tuition rates are at the 90th percentile and the program costs are not. Basic skill and academic courses are low-cost programs, less costly than the areas his program ignores, such as homemaking, shop and physical education. The government deserves a better reputation for its full, and as-yet-unquestioned, funding of the school than Mr. Swenson gives it. Mr. Swenson is responsible for correcting this misperception.

Recommendations for Further Action:

Mr. Swenson has demonstrated his ability to produce the kind of results that are expected in his school, and more. He should be able to make the required improvements that are stated under heading numbers 1, 3 and 5 (in the immediately preceding paragraphs). He should accomplish these improvements within one year.

Recommendation 1: Until these improvements are made, I recommend that no further increase in tuition be granted.

Recommendation 2: When the current contract expires, I recommend the government include a new provision requiring a biannual financial audit.

Signed by: Mr. Results

This concludes the results-based evaluation. Mr. Results could not take the actions he felt were appropriate; he could only recommend those actions. Superintendents share this condition in many public school settings, where board ratification is required before action can be carried out. It is a serious limitation when administrators have to evaluate others, make recommendations and risk not being backed up; particularly when they will have to face the evaluated person in the future, maybe year after year.

When readers compare their evaluations and recommendations with the evaluation document written by Mr. Results, they may find the differences—or the similarities—surprising.

The experience of presenting Mr. Results' results-based evaluation helps to demonstrate one of the most important aspects of personnel evaluation and personnel evaluation systems. There are many viewpoints from which to judge, and as a result, individual evaluators make judgments of cases, each in his or her own way.

5

Performance-Based Principal Evaluation

This chapter presents the evaluation philosophy of the advocate, Mr. Performance, who is committed to making an evaluation that is "performance-based." As with Mr. Results, the advocate in the last chapter, Mr. Performance is not searching for an answer to how he should evaluate school principals. He feels confident that he already knows how.

PART 1
EVALUATING THE PERFORMANCE

The Only Rational Basis for Evaluating a Principal

The only ethical way to evaluate a school principal is to evaluate his or her work "performance." Performance-based principal evaluation systems are forthright, show respect for the integrity of principals and respond to public expectations.

Performance is the actual work that principals do, their work behavior. The criteria for judging the work behavior of a principal can be divided into four work behavior categories:

1. Leadership traits exhibited in the position;
2. Management skills exhibited in the position;
3. Knowledge utilized in carrying out the position;
4. Individual actions as compared with the personal qualities and traits required in the position.

All personnel evaluation systems grow from a desire to improve institutional performance. The greater objective of evaluating educators is to benefit students; to improve the quality and amount that students learn. A completed performance-based evaluation scheme allows for the possibility of putting the assessment of school outcomes to work in an ethical and responsible way. It uses measures of student and school performance to pinpoint the needs that the principal should address. The principal's evaluator uses outcome data to assess school and student needs, and based on those assessments, directs the principal's performance behavior.

The point is, according to Mr. Performance, that all personnel evaluations are designed to reinforce some behaviors and to change certain others.

The competing approach to school principal evaluation, results-based evaluation (as discussed in Chapter Four), ignores two realities that control the actions of principals, and therefore, set the limits of their true accountability.

The first is an insufficient base of "hard" professional knowledge, the kind of hard knowledge scientists use to make decisions with highly predictable results (one critical example is that we do not know exactly how learning occurs in human beings).

The second is the limited options that principals have for exercising their own judgment, freely. Constituent demands and employer restrictions shrink principals' fields of choice significantly, and therefore, any sense of fairness dictates that evaluations of school principals must be conducted with a full consideration of their narrow span of decision options. Also, the best option (the one which promises the best results) may not be available to a principal for any of several reasons. (The same, or similar, limitations apply to practitioners in other professions such as medicine, law and engineering, as well.

And "performance" measurement is THE method of accountability practiced in them. Professions hold their members accountable for performing work that meets and matches the current professional standards.)

The results-based approach to making written evaluation reports assumes that measured school outcomes provide accurate and sufficient bases for principal evaluation. However, there are two questionable assumptions associated with the results-based approach. One assumption is that all the desired outcomes can be achieved by someone. The second assumption (related to the first assumption) is that whoever knows how to achieve all the desired outcomes will also be free to act totally according to his or her own judgment. The consequence of these assumptions is that the results-based evaluator will keep changing principals until one is found who can do the job to the satisfaction of the evaluator. Taking this approach to its extreme, there may be expressed outcomes that are actually unattainable. Also, no principal can truly act with complete freedom.

In spite of a certain simplistic appeal, the results-based approach trivializes two major facts. First, the fact that the way learning occurs is not known, and second, the fact that the way a person makes up his mind is not known. Something is known about these matters, but not enough to control their outcomes. Holding a principal responsible for student learning, given these facts, defies any sense of fairness. (Although there are certain areas having to do with learning over which principals can have control. For example, the provision or denial of suitable environments or learning media. Today's knowledge base is insufficient to make principals the guarantors of all school outcomes.)

Principals

Principals work in a political setting and are subjected to the same transient, fluctuating vicissitudes that characterize all dealings with people. Seldom is a clear consensus on objectives reached. State laws dealing with school purposes range from deliberate oversimplification to ponderous obfuscation. The political factor takes on added importance at the highest management levels of a school system. School boards and superintendents change every few years, and each change brings some alteration in district priorities. This stands in remarkable contrast to private sector institutions which tend to be very stable at the top, with the same major priorities and goals remaining in clear focus for many years.

Beyond the school system level are state and national school politics. The law has expanded the authority, for who will participate in making school level decisions to such an extent that individual accountability for school outcomes is impossible? Shared accountability for school results is now an implicit condition. Nearly everyone associated with schools, (parents, politicians, educators, citizens, even students), understands the complexity of the institution and can see the futility of holding one person accountable for the overall results.

Nevertheless, the public does have an absolute right to expect and demand employee accountability. The public recognizes its right to hold employees accountable for doing their jobs well. It is entitled to have school principals performing their jobs in a manner that is consistent with high professional standards.

Adopting a performance-based principal evaluation system puts a proper focus on the evaluation process for both principals and their evaluators. Performance will be monitored and the evaluator's judgments will be limited to performance factors.

Mr. Performance admits it may be true that evaluation judgments are nothing more than the opinions of the particular evaluator, and if one evaluator is replaced by another, some significant changes in judgments can occur. But this condition is inherent in all personnel evaluation. It should not be interpreted to mean that personnel evaluation is inescapably insubstantial, a will-o'-the-wisp phenomenon. The actual number of personnel actions a school system takes (promotions, demotions, warnings, letters of recognition) are always a function of district leadership and legal requirements. Adopting a performance-based system neither adds to nor subtracts from the number of possible personnel actions (promotions, demotions, and others). The performance-based system will, however, establish a clear and defensible record of the evidence and judgments that might have led to any subsequent actions for, or against, a principal.

Some school administrators believe that performance-based evaluation is appropriate only for teachers and not for managers; that it is appropriate to hold teachers accountable for following procedures adopted by school systems and to hold school managers accountable for school outcomes and overall school success. They maintain that school systems have failed to focus on results and hold school administrators accountable for results to the detriment of the nation's interests. Such school administrators insist that all managers are accountable for institutional outcomes; otherwise they are not true managers, and school systems that fail to hold principals accountable for school outcomes are not treating principals as true managers.

The premise that principal evaluation based on outcomes determines whether or not principals are managers is ill-founded. Principals are managers in the truest sense of the word; they "manage" their schools but don't "create" them. They create "school environments" by the way they manage, but they don't create the student bodies in those environments.

Everyone associated with the schools is concerned about improved outcomes. No one group can make special claim to that objective. At the same time, no two groups can agree on a definition of those outcomes, to say nothing about their inability to agree on standards.

Performance standards for school principals have been established and are being used as the bases for holding principals accountable within principal evaluation systems. Such evaluation systems are rational, defensible, and lead to improved school outcomes.

Whose job is it to see that a school produces results? It is a responsibility shared by the people involved (beginning with those who make the laws and allocate the dollars through to those who do the teaching). But the question remains, "What is to be gained by holding a building principal responsible if the students in his or her school show poor results?" The principal merely becomes a scapegoat if this happens; nothing is accomplished, and the students continue to suffer.

All school systems that want to improve their schools should not wait another generation before intelligently clarifying what they mean by principal's accountability. Mr. Performance would argue for a full compliment of principal performance standards. Otherwise, further delay in defining principal accountability will prolong the arrival of the day when real improvement occurs in their schools.

Readers should ask themselves if the principals in their communities are confused about their accountability. In the communities that have invested the resources to produce a well developed set of "performance objectives" for principals, the principals will not be confused. In communities where this has not been done, readers should ask: "Why hasn't it been done?"

PART 2—CRITERIA

Mr. Performance describes the criteria used in his version of a performance-based principal evaluation system under the following headings:

1. Leadership traits required of principals;

2. Management skills required of principals;

3. Knowledge required to carry out principals' roles;

4. Individual actions as compared with the personal qualities and traits required in the principal position.

[Note: Readers are encouraged to write these four headings on a separate piece of paper, and briefly note the major concepts they think should be included under each of these topics. While reading this section, readers may want to write additional comments that reflect their individual preferences. After completing Part 2, readers may then compare their outlines with the system Mr. Performance has advocated. This activity will help readers to identify which of the approaches, results-based or performance-based principal evaluation, that they prefer for making principal evaluations.]

The Criteria for Judging Principal Performance

The four general criteria used in a performance-based system can generate a long list of performance objectives. Constructing such a list is worthwhile because its contents help to pinpoint accountability. Likewise, once a complete list of performance objectives is established, there is no need to evaluate every principal on every performance objective at every evaluation time, but it is essential to evaluate each principal according to each general criterion. Readers will recall the points made earlier about successful principal evaluation systems pinpointing individual principal accountability by specifying the criteria for making evaluative judgments; and successful principal evaluation systems also adapt to the individual being evaluated.

Adapting the performance-based evaluation to an individual principal occurs by pre-selecting the performance objectives that the individual's evaluation will focus on during a specific evaluation cycle. The common expectation is that the evaluation system will be applied uniformly, not identically. Using selected performance objectives, some from within "each general criterion," meets the requirement for conducting a uniform evaluation system. Using some performance objectives (again, from each of the criteria headings) also meets the test of individual adaptability.

Mr. Performance will now present a discussion of the criteria he believes to be the foundation of a performance-based principal evaluation system. He identified these under four headings stated above. His more complete explanation of each one follows.

Leadership Traits

The role of school principal is a leadership position. The following is a description of leadership criteria appropriate for judging a principal's performance.

Leadership: Judgment

Tacitus, a Roman historian, said, "Reason and judgment are the foundations of leadership." Nothing will lead a principal into trouble faster than faulty reasoning and bad judgment.

Exercising intelligent judgment and reason involves conceptual ability, seeing broad inter-relationships, foresight, and "common sense logic." These are qualities that (for most people) can and do improve with age and experience. To some degree, training can contribute to the development of good reasoning and good judgment, as can the influence of mentors and models.

Leadership: Communication

Communication skills are indispensable aspects of leadership. These are not mere language arts skills. They are clarity and credibility. Moses, one of history's greatest leaders, is reported to have had a speech impediment, yet the messages he delivered serve as foundations for western civilization. His messages were clear and credible.

Clarity: Clear messages are framed within a syntax (choice of words and phrases) that matches the audience. The delivery method influences clarity, and effective communicators select the right words to convey their meaning, the right medium for their message.

Credibility: The principal's communication purposes are to 1) convey information, 2) motivate, and 3) promote understanding and cooperation. Credible messages are constructed so that the audience can recognize the honesty of the message and its relationship to their lives.

Leadership: Style

Three aspects of leadership style notably impact the principal's role: 1) task-oriented behavior versus people-oriented behavior (task-oriented people always focus on the demands for getting tasks completed, and people-oriented people always focus on what people demand); 2) holding on to power versus giving it up (an autocratic leader delegates nothing, whereas a "laissez-faire" leader abdicates his authority); 3) confronting conflict versus running away from it. These personal orientations are presented graphically by the following:

TASK ←——————→ RELATIONSHIPS

AUTOCRAT ←——————→ LAISSEZ-FAIRE

FIGHT ←——————————→ FLIGHT

Each person's temperament pulls him toward one side or the other of each continuum. Successful leaders can be found leaning in either direction in the categories, even changing from one side to the other when appropriate, and usually avoiding the extremes.

Successful leaders balance realities and possibilities; the goal is kept in sight and the people kept in mind. At the same time, leaders are goal-oriented. They will even endure periods of unpopularity for the sake of achieving institutional goals.

Successful leaders skillfully utilize the strengths of their associates, and they help those strengths to grow. However, autocrats bring no one along with them, because they do not involve people, they direct them; they are prima donnas with egos that require all the recognition. At the other extreme, laissez-faire practitioners wait for the group to find its own direction.

Effective leaders act decisively, but not hastily. They take risks, and they have the courage to carry out their convictions.

Management Skills

Principals are managers, and the following is a description of the criteria appropriate for judging a principal's management behavior.

Management Skills: Planning

Whatever else management may include, goal-setting and the design of plans to gain the achievement of these goals is a primary activity. Every successful manager knows the excitement of having brought a group together through a goal-setting experience and the resultant satisfaction of having everyone take personal credit for having set the goal.

A principal is responsible for numerous plans: student achievement, cafeteria operation, maintenance, safety, health, discipline, budgets, communications, public relations, district relations, and more. The essence of planning is making choices, and since all resources are scarce, good judgment demands discretion.

Management Skills: Organizing

Even the best laid plans often go awry, if they were not well-organized. Organizing includes all of the activities which precede implementing the plan.

Managers are responsible for turning plans into action. The first steps involve organizing the environment. Assigning staff is one such organizing action. Arranging for the necessary equipment, materials, and work spaces are further organizing actions. Sequencing and coordinating events to insure a successful flow of activity are organizing actions.

Preparing the staff so it understands purposes, expectations, individual responsibilities and combined responsibilities also requires organization.

Management Skills: Supervising

The title "principal" comes from an earlier time when the position was originally created. Then, the designated head or first teacher in a school was called the "principal teacher." The job of supervising staff members, directing their efforts, and evaluating their performance remains the principal's primary responsibility.

Supervision includes asigning work, ratifying the teachers' plans, assisting teachers in meeting their objectives, monitoring performance, making suggestions, and providing in-service training. All of these are part of the supervision process. The principal is also responsible for judging the quality of his subordinates' work.

Management Skills: Controlling

Controlling is the ability to make needed adjustments at the earliest possible moment. A predetermined set of continuing measures and assessments are required to maintain management control of an organization. Each area of the principal's responsibility requires the exercise of control.

An efficient school control system follows three principles:

1. Data is collected unobtrusively (wherever possible, the data is created as a normal part of operations as the work is accomplished).
2. Data is collected regularly.
3. Data is shared with others who need it.

Knowledge

The position of school principal is a complex one. Principals wear three hats at once for three areas of responsibility and must be knowledgeable i each area. They are educators, public officials and managers. Principals must be knowledgeable in each of the three areas. Being knowledgeable is not the same thing as having sound judgment. It involves possessing a body of established knowledge that exists within each area.

Knowledge: Education

Learning Theory: Learning theory applications permeate the school environment. Principals must act on the basis of their knowledge of learning theories, attitude shaping, motivation theories, group and individual behaviors, and cultural influences.

Instruction: The primary responsibility of a school principal is supervision of the teaching staff and its instructional efforts. It isn't always possible for principals to know the content of each course taught in the school, but they do need to know sound pedagogy.

Curriculum: Principals should be familiar with all of the programs in their schools, know the curriculum objectives in their schools, and know the methods and categories for measurement.

District Organization and Services: No school is capable of serving everyone. The special needs of some individual students and staff are beyond the scope of any single administrator. Principals need to know about the programs and resources that are available within the school system or through state or regional arrangements.

Knowledge: Legal

Law: All principals need a more than rudimentary knowledge of the laws that effect the operation of a school: laws governing safety and student welfare are one kind; "due process law" is another; student, staff, and parent rights a third. Few school administrators have any legal training beyond the minimal licensing requirements, and that means the most significant practical legal knowledge for principals is the ability to recognize when they need legal help.

Policy: Principals are accountable for knowing the policies in operation in their school systems. Governing school boards may well be the "brains" that guide the school systems, but principals are the "fingers" of those bodies; the means to carry out the brains' intentions.

Collective Bargaining: Principals in school systems that operate under a collective bargaining agreement must know the terms and provisions of the labor agreements between the employing school system and the labor unions who represent the school system's employees. The teacher's labor agreement (contract) is the dominant legal document in the life of a principal. As much as 90 percent of a teacher contract will deal with matters that are directly related to principals' assigned areas of responsibility.

Knowledge: Self

"Know thyself," said Socrates. Principals need to know some things about their own personalities that others, in positions with less responsibility, may never really need to know about themselves. Every principal needs to know the following things about himself or herself as an individual:

1. His or her primary method of working with others, and the weaknesses in that method;
2. His or her own individual fears as principal;
3. His or her own individual strengths as principal;
4. How he or she confronts principal conflicts as an individual;
5. What makes him or her angry as an individual;
6. How the individual principal expresses anger;
7. What the individual principal's vanity points are;
8. What the individual principal's emotional relationships with "power" are;
9. Whom the individual principal trusts;
10. The aspects of the individual principal's character that make him or her vulnerable to those who will try to use him or her;
11. How and whether the individual principal effectively shows concern for others.

Inevitably, people in power positions will face a challenge, and the challenge may be quite personal. The principal must be prepared to face challenges and cope with them.

Personality Traits

The published descriptions of outstanding principals, such as those contained in Sarah Lawrence Lightfoot's book, *The Good High School*, demonstrate that there are many personality types to go along with the accolade, "good principal."

All good principals seem to have in common some combination of six personality traits, or personal qualities: honesty, self-confidence, responsibility, empathy, tolerance, and vitality. The presence of each of these qualities in abundance is necessary in the make-up of all effective principals. These qualities and their definitions should be included as criteria in any scheme for evaluating school principals.

Personality: Honesty

The first ingredient of honesty is truthfulness, the second is trust. Trust is essential to effective administration. Good principals know this and never take it for granted that trust will be maintained without their effort. They are sensitive to the circumstances where misunderstandings are apt to occur and make special efforts to prevent their occurrence.

Personality: Self-confidence

Good principals expect success, not just for themselves, but for their students and staff as well. Their positive attitude shows up in their having senses of humor, and more importantly, in the quality of their working relationships. Good principals are emotionally resilient, can cope with their own lonely hours and the personal traumas that come to them on a daily basis.

Personality: Responsibility

When Harry Truman put his "The Buck Stops Here" sign on his desk, it was more than a personal reminder; it reminded everyone of his awesome responsibilities, and it conveyed the notion that he relished them. Being responsible requires the courage to take a chance. Taking responsibility for anything includes an element of risk, and when people assume responsibility for their own and other people's actions, their risks increase. Good principals are not just willing to accept responsibility—they seek it out and welcome it.

Personality: Empathy

People have dimensions to their lives beyond work. They have accomplishments and they have aspirations beyond their achievements. Almost every day principals are confronted by someone asking for, and expecting, consideration for some "special need." An unsympathetic manner leads to lowered staff morale and less enthusiastic workers. Although principals cannot grant every request, they can maintain their empathy.

Personality: Tolerance

People know when they are accorded respect. They recognize tolerant treatment and expect it. On the other hand, everyone is reputed to have some prejudices—race and sex prejudice are just two kinds. Good principals may not be entirely free of prejudice, but they will have rationally examined their own prejudices and will deliberately strive to not act upon them.

Personality: Vitality

Being energetic is not the same as cheerleading, but it is infectious. Administrative roles require energy over and above that for most positions. Principals set a tone for their schools by how they themselves work. Their productivity influences the staff's productivity.

[NOTE: Appendix B addresses specific performance-based objectives which can be used by evaluators of school principals. Before readers turn to Appendix B, they are urged to take a moment to write down two things: first, a short list of performance criteria, and then under each criterion, write down one or two behavioral statements that are considered to be essential as principal behavior. This exercise will help readers compare their concepts of performance objectives with those developed by Mr. Performance in advocating the concept.

The performance objectives listed in Appendix B are based on accumulated practical knowledge of experienced principal evaluators and a considerable body of educational literature that associates specific principal behaviors with the success of schools.

No maker of such lists ever thinks his list is the ultimate list, and this list is no exception. Each school district should assume the responsibility for developing its own set of performance objectives, however similar they might be to some other set of objectives. Doing this is the best way to assure that there will be a common understanding about the evaluation system between the principal and the evaluator. Understanding leads to commitment and confidence in the system, without which the system will fail.]

PART 3—EXAMINING THE CASE STUDY DATA FOR A PERFORMANCE-BASED EVALUATION

[NOTE: Mr. Performance follows the same steps in carrying out his evaluation of Mr. Swenson, the case study principal, as did Mr. Results in Chapter Four.]

Mr. Performance's Report

This is a "Base Line" performance evaluation of Mr. John Swenson, Principal of the International School. All data were gathered by the evaluator, through direct observation and oral reports collected during a three-day, on-site visit.

Data

The following data were useful in determining "standards" for the school and pinpointing the principal's performance needs and his accomplishments.

3. Grades: Kindergarten through grade eight

4. Enrollment: two hundred students

10. Most students stay two years, a few stay three years, and only two or three students stay four years, none longer.

11. Fifty percent of the students are American, the others are from more than a dozen nations (most come from European and Middle Eastern countries).

13. The contract requires a mainstream U.S. public school program for all students.

14. Students are expected to make their normal gains in performance and achievement while attending the school.

30. Students appear to be above grade in their basic language and math skills, and most academic courses.

31. Student achievement in science (grades seven and eight) appears to be below school standards.

36. All students are capable of working in a regular school program.

40. An unqualified teacher teaches upper grade science.

46. Recruiting teachers to the school is difficult.

49. Tuition costs are at the ninetieth percentile of similar contract schools.

54. The community is composed of water specialists and their families, including scientists, technicians, and laborers.

The following data were considered useful in evaluating the principal's "performance." Items marked with a double asterisk (**) were most useful, items marked with a single asterisk (*) were of secondary value, items listed without an asterisk were considered only slightly valuable, and some data items were ignored because they were considered irrelevant to "performance-based" evaluation.

5.** Staff:

(a) eleven regular classroom teachers

(b) one reading specialist

(c) one resource teacher

(d) one assistant principal

(e) one principal/chief administrator

(f) two secretaries

(g) eight parent volunteer classroom aides

(Class size/staff size equals the average of similar schools.)

15.** The school goals are understood and accepted by the staff and community.

16.** The school program emphasizes basic skills and academics.

17.** Art, music and physical education instruction are conducted by the regular classroom teachers.

18.** No shop, homemaking, typing or similar courses exist.

19.** No standardized testing program is in place.

20.** Student progress is assessed by teacher and principal observation in all curriculum areas.

21.* The principal has agreed to use standardized tests of basic skills in the future, and with the American students only.

22.* The school has a twenty station computer lab.

23.* Computer software is acquired from the public domain at little or no cost.

24.* The third and fifth grade teachers use the computer lab according to their own interests.

25.** No current plans exist to integrate the computer lab into the regular program.

26.* The school needs playground and Physical Education equipment.

27.* The school has adequate instructional supplies and materials.

28. Staff members conduct some after school programs for students.

29.* The school atmosphere reflects high levels of cooperation at both the student and staff levels.

32.* No conflict between students of any age group is evident.

33.* The school has not had a serious student or staff member accident.

34.* Minor student accidents (bumps and bruises) are at a minimum.

35.** Students appear to be working hard at their studies.

37.** Staff members appear to be working hard at their jobs.

38.* Staff members are provided annual in-service education.

39. All school personnel act friendly toward each other and visitors.

41.* Staff members respect the principal.

42.* Staff members do not take their complaints to the principal.

43.* Some staff members complain privately about a work overload.

44.** Forty-seven percent of the professional staff, including the principal, are members of the same small religious sect.

45.** An acknowledged incompetent teacher was allowed to remain in the classroom for an entire school year without being re-assigned or dismissed.

47.* The principal has expensive computer and television equipment in his office for his own use.

48.* The principal reports a small contingency reserve.

51.* No employer has complained about tuition rates or refused or delayed payment.

52. The principal's residence is supported out of school funds in accordance with the school contract.

53.** The principal reports that he has saved the school thousands of operating dollars because of his frugality.

Community Description:

55.** The great majority of parents are openly supportive of the school although they do want:

55.1 A regular standardized testing program for American students

55.2 An advisory group to review the school budget.

56. The principal's home is one of the two best houses in the community.

57. A small group of parents have formally complained about:

57.1 Religious imbalance of the staff

57.2 An unqualified upper grade science teacher

57.3 Inadequate Physical Education equipment

57.4 Inadequate after school programs for students

57.5 Failure to dismiss an incompetent teacher midyear due to poor budgeting for contingencies

57.6 Excessive funds used to support the principal's residence.

Principal Description:

58.* Credentialed English teacher and school administrator

59.* "Thoreau-like" (self-existing) personality, limited social skills

60.** Considered unapproachable by staff

61.** Regards himself as the local expert on school priorities

62. Has no close friends

63.* Hard worker

64.** Poor personnel recruiting skills (relies on staff members to recruit their friends)

65.** Careful of money to the point of being penurious

66.* Devotee of Mastery Learning

67.* Experienced in nonstandard and overseas school operation and management

68.** Asks for advice from those he respects, does not want unsolicited advice

69.** Strong dislike for criticism, reduces school complaints to personality defects in the critic

70.* Justifies his actions as being appropriate to his contract

The evaluator has ranked the data and clustered it according to the four general criteria described earlier.

Leadership Qualities Required in the Position:

15.** The school goals are understood and accepted by the staff and community.

35.** Students appear to be working hard at their studies.

37.** Staff members appear to be working hard at their jobs.

55.** The great majority of parents are openly supportive of the school, although they do want:

55.1 A regular standardized testing program for American students

55.2 An advisory group to review the school budget

29.* The school atmosphere reflects high levels of cooperation at both the student and staff levels.

32.* No conflict between students of any age group is apparent.

41.* Staff members appear to respect the principal.

42.* Staff members do not take their complaints to the principal.

43.* Some staff members complain privately about a work overload.

51.* No employer has complained about tuition rates or refused or delayed payment.

Management Skills Required in the Position:

5.** Staff:

(a) eleven regular classroom teachers

(b) one reading specialist

(c) one resource teacher

(d) one assistant principal

(e) one principal/chief administrator

(f) two secretaries

(g) eight parent volunteer classroom aides

(Class size: staff size equals the average of similar schools.)

25.** No current plans exist to integrate the computer lab into the regular program.

44.** Forty-seven percent of the professional staff, including the principal, are members of the same small religious sect.

45.** An acknowledged incompetent teacher was allowed to remain in the classroom for an entire school year without being reassigned or dismissed.

53.** The principal reports that he has saved the school thousands of operating dollars because of his frugality.

22.* The school has a twenty station computer lab.

24.* The third and fifth grade teachers use the computer lab according to their own interests.

26.* The school needs playground and Physical Education equipment.

27.* The school has adequate instructional supplies and materials.

29.* The school atmosphere reflects high levels of cooperation at both the student and staff levels.

32.* No conflict between students of any age group is apparent.

33.* The school has not had a serious student or staff member accident.

34.* Minor student accidents (bumps and bruises) are at a minimal level.

38.* Staff members are provided annual in-service education.

47.* The principal has expensive computer and television equipment in his office for his own use.

Knowledge Required in the Position:

16.** The school program emphasizes basic skills and academics.

17.** Art, music, and physical education instruction are conducted by the regular classroom teachers.

18.** No shop, homemaking, typing, or similar courses exist.

19.** No standardized testing program is in place.

20.** Student progress is assessed by teacher and principal observation in all curriculum areas.

23.* Computer software is acquired from the public domain at little or no cost.

58.* Credentialed English teacher and school administrator

66.* Devotee of Mastery Learning

67.* Experienced in nonstandard and overseas school operation and management

Personal Qualities or Traits Required in the Position:

60.** Considered unapproachable by staff

61.** Regards himself as the local expert on school priorities

64.** Poor personnel recruiting skills

65.** Careful of money to the point of being penurious

68.** Asks for advise from those he respects, does not want unsolicited advice

69.** Strong dislike for criticism, reduces school complaints to personality defects in the critic

59.* "Thoreau" personality (self-existing), limited social skills

63.* Hard worker

70.* Justifies his actions as being appropriate to his contract

The Written Evaluation

[NOTE: Mr. Performance will use what he has seen and heard to focus his evaluation on the four major work behavior criteria categories he identified earlier:

1. Leadership traits exhibited in the position;
2. Management skills exhibited in the position;
3. Knowledge utilized in carrying out the position;
4. Individual actions as compared with the personal qualities and traits required in the position.]

Mr. Performance's Written Evaluation

Dated this date
From: Mr. Performance
To: The Overseas Education Officer
Subject: John Swenson Evaluation

Background Data:

Mr. Swenson is the principal of the International School, located somewhere in North America. He has been in this position for seven years.

School Standards and Principal Performance Expectations:

The school includes grades kindergarten through eight. There are no handicapped students. The school has a high turnover rate among students. The parents are middle to upper middle class scientific and technical workers.

The school serves most students for two years, during which time they are assured a mainstream U.S. public school education and are expected to make normal achievement growth.

The basic skills and academic programs (with the exception of upper grade science) produce good results, as witnessed by direct observation, but without supportive test data to confirm the observation. Specific courses in physical education and activity courses (typing, homemaking, computer literacy) do not exist in the school.

Teacher recruitment is difficult here due to its remote location, and no teacher candidate pool exists. An unqualified teacher was allowed to remain in the school well after the time when the incompetency was discovered.

No conditions in the school warrant setting or accepting anything but normal U.S. performance standards for students or the principal.

Findings and Judgments:

1. **Leadership**: Mr. Swenson is an able leader. The parents, students, and staff enthusiastically pursue the traditional academic goals of a good school, as evidenced by

their hard work and continued cooperation. Mr. Swenson takes criticism in stride, while holding to his convictions.

2. **Management**: The school operates smoothly in spite of some important management deficiencies. The school's safety record is outstanding, but the facility needs more and better physical education equipment. A personal computer lab exists without a plan for effective utilization. The staffing pattern is adequate in number, but not well-designed for student needs; a resource teacher and a reading specialist may be superfluous to high-achieving students when they are denied other specialty courses commonly found in U.S. schools. The school is more than adequately funded, so there is no shortage of resources to address these needs.

   The regular faculty (other than local hires) is predominantly made up of members of the same small religious sect, which calls into question how much religious influence they may have on students. This condition should be corrected during next year's recruitment efforts.

   Mr. Swenson is commended for providing regular in-service education to his staff, something that is often difficult for administrators in remote locations. He went to considerable expense in bringing a specialist in Mastery Learning techniques to the school who offered a full week's in-service training to all professional staff members.

3. **Knowledge**: Mr. Swenson is technically qualified for his position. The school program appears to come from his priorities, as evidenced by his strong leadership. The scope of the program is too narrow, and Mr. Swenson needs to become more knowledgeable about the requirements of a good upper grade elementary school program.

4. **Personal Qualities**: Mr. Swenson holds people at a distance, which inhibits the amount of timely and candid feedback he receives. This slows down his response time for making necessary changes in the school. He has a preoccupation with saving money, which interferes with his ability to plan and allocate resources well.

   Mr. Swenson has a near-perfect temperament for working in this location. His community and staff recognize this important ingredient as a part of his effectiveness and are appreciative of his efforts.

Recommendations for Further Action:

Mr. Swenson has demonstrated that given the right knowledge and management skills, he can lead the International School to competently perform at expected standards.

He will have to improve his knowledge of the curriculum and testing programs that are expected of U.S. schools and make the necessary program additions. He needs to make better use of the personal computers purchased for classroom use. He should expand the school program to offer subjects that are lacking.

He must recruit new staff members to correct the religious imbalance.

He needs to improve his planning and staffing skills in order to better serve his students and to insure that there will be no repetition of maintaining an incompetent staff member for an unnecessarily long time.

I recommend that no further tuition increases be granted until there is evidence of improvement.

I recommend that a follow-up evaluation be conducted in one year.

Signed by: Mr. Performance

Readers must have noticed that Mr. Performance listed only the data he considers relevant to his "performance" evaluation. His first group of data established his concept of school standards, and his second group of data constituted the "performance" evaluation data Mr. Performance used in his evaluation of Mr. Swenson. (The numbers in front of each item corresponded to the numbers used in the original DATA LIST.)

Readers are likely to have some disagreements with what Mr. Performance chose to ignore and possibly some of the things he considered highly important. Such is the nature of personnel evaluation. Each evaluator is responsible for his or her own judgments, those items that they attend to and those items that they ignore. Mr. Performance focused on the things he felt would lead to improvements in the International School.

6

Comparing the Two Evaluation Systems

Reviewing a principal's past evaluations isn't an absolute must. However, past evaluations, if available, do reveal something about their subject. A series of past evaluations may indicate something about a principal's past progress and development. If past evaluations were done by the present evaluator, they are a record of both the principal's work and the evaluator's work. If past evaluations were written by another evaluator, those evaluations reflect the principal's expectations and understanding regarding his or her own evaluation. For these reasons evaluators are advised to review each principal's past evaluations, both the ones they have written and those written by others. Remember that the written evaluation is there for a third party to read and judge. The third party is judging both the principal's competency and the sufficiency of the evaluator's work.

The Process

If Mr. Results and Mr. Performance actually had been the imagined Mr. Swenson's evaluators, they would have had access to identical information and information sources. Each advocate represents a hypothetical extreme, yet each would have followed a similar process:

1. Both Mr. Results and Mr. Performance were responsible for conducting an evaluation of the (fictional) International

School and for making recommendations to the government. (In Chapters Four and Five, respectively, each advocate/evaluator described his rationale and approach to making principal evaluations.)

2. In their reports both advocates/evaluators described the general criteria they would use, and each relied on his own concept of a standard, middle class U.S. school as the basis for comparing his findings with his standard of expectation for a school. The results-based evaluator (Mr. Results) focused on school outcomes, and the performance-based evaluator (Mr. Performance) focused on the principal's behavior.
3. Each used data gathered first hand through personal observations in making the evaluation.
4. Each gathered his own data through direct school observation and by talking with people associated with the school.
5. Each judged the data according to his own criteria.
6. Both evaluators submitted written evaluations which described their judgments and the evidence used to support those judgments. Both written evaluations included recommendations for action that the evaluator believed to be appropriate to the situation.

Comparison of the Data Items Used in the Two Evaluations

Mr. Results used 25 data items, selected from the DATA LIST, in his evaluation. Item 18, "no shop, homemaking, typing, or similar courses," appeared twice under two of his five individual criteria headings: "gc1. results" and "gc3. goals and purposes."

The performance-based evaluator used 42 data items in his evaluation. Item 32, "no evident conflict between students of any age group," was used twice under two of his criteria headings: "Leadership" and "Management" skills.

Twelve data items were used by both evaluators. The following seven items were judged "most important" by both evaluators:

15. The school goals are understood and accepted by the staff and community.
18. No shop, homemaking, typing, or similar courses exist.
19. No standardized testing program is in place.
34. Minor student accidents (bumps and bruises) are at a minimal level.
35. Students appear to be working hard at their studies.
37. Staff members appear to be working hard at their jobs.
44. Forty-seven percent of the professional staff, including the principal, are members of the same small religious sect.

One item was judged "important" by both evaluators:

51. No employer has complained about tuition rates or refused or delayed payment.

Four items were considered important to each evaluator, but the evaluators differed in their opinions about the value of each item:

27. The school has adequate instructional supplies and materials. (most valuable to "performance" evaluation)
29. The school atmosphere reflects high levels of cooperation at both the student and staff levels.
(most valuable to "results" evaluation)
32. No conflict between students of any age group exists.
(most valuable to "results" evaluation)
33. The school has not had a serious student or staff member accident. (most valuable to "results" evaluation)

Comparison of Findings and Judgments

PE Task 13: Comparing Readers' Data with Data Used in the Examples

Readers should compare the data items on their PE Task 11 lists to the data items in the "results-based" evaluation (at the end of Chapter Four). Likewise, they should compare their lists to see how many items match those in the "performance-based" evaluation (at the end of Chapter Five). Readers whose lists match more of one model list than the other reveal a clear preference for one type of data over the other. Also, the similarities suggest that readers have a clear preference for one style of evaluation over the other.

DO PE TASK 13 NOW

Using the twelve prioritized items from the DATA LIST developed in PE Task 11, readers should compare and count the number of matching items that were given the highest importance rating by Mr. Results; then do the same count and comparison with the items ranked by Mr. Performance as being of highest importance. An examination of the two evaluations reveals what each evaluator found commendable about Mr. Swenson and his operation.

Mr. Results commended:

1. The school's outstanding safety record
2. High levels of understanding and support of school goals
3. Hard work of students and staff
4. Community support

Mr. Performance commended:

1. Mr. Swenson's leadership ability
    1.1. Support for the school's academic goals
    1.2. Hard-working students and staff
2. The school operates smoothly in spite of some management deficiencies.
3. Mr. Swenson provides regular staff in-service training.
4. Mr. Swenson's personal temperament is well-suited to the job and is appreciated by the staff and community.

Deficiencies Found by the Two Evaluators

Mr. Results found these deficiencies:

1. Upper grade science achievement was low.
2. No standardized testing program.
3. No non-academic courses.
4. Legitimate negative impressions are ignored.
5. Possible religious indoctrination of students.
6. Impression that funds are limited.

Mr. Results wants these deficiencies corrected, including the impressions that students are possibly being religiously indoctrinated and that school funds are limited. He does not say how any deficiency is to be corrected, just that Mr. Swenson appears competent to correct these things in one year.

Mr. Performance found these deficiencies:

1. Inadequate Physical Education equipment
2. No plan for effective use of computer lab
3. Staffing pattern is inadequate.

4. Religious imbalance of staff
5. School curriculum is too narrow.
6. No standardized testing program
7. Mr. Swenson is unapproachable.

Mr. Performance wants to correct these deficiencies as follows:

1. Mr. Swenson should order and install Physical Education equipment.
2. Mr. Swenson should develop and carry out an effective plan for the computer lab.
3. Mr. Swenson should improve his recruiting skills.
4. Mr. Swenson should become more knowledgeable about the scope of a good school program.
5. Mr. Swenson should become more knowledgeable about school testing programs.
6. Mr. Swenson should improve his planning and staffing skills.

Mr. Performance suggested that the solutions to the deficiencies will most likely emerge from improving the knowledge and skills of Mr. Swenson in each of the six areas where a deficiency was noted. He specifically calls for a follow-up evaluation in one year.

PE Task 14: Comparing the Findings and Judgments of the Two Examples

DO PE TASK 14 NOW

Readers should make and record their own comparisons of the "Findings and Judgments" of the two evaluators. They should consider and do the following:

1. Write the numbers of those items that both Mr. Results and Mr. Performance cited.

2. Use two lists to write the numbers of the items about which the "Findings" were different. Write the results-based item numbers first, then write the performance-based numbers.

3. Decide if the evaluators appeared to make different or similar conclusions about their findings. Readers should write brief comments about their decisions. Some suitable example comments follow:

   Both evaluators are concerned about the lack of a standardized testing program in the school. They had similar findings:

   Both evaluators are concerned about the religious imbalance of the regular staff. Mr. Results wants to dispense with any impression of religious indoctrination of students. Mr. Performance wants the principal to change the make-up of the staff. Both found the area to be appropriate for concern.

   Mr. Results wants non-academic courses introduced into the school. Mr.Performance wants the school program expanded. Both are dealing with the same concern. However, Mr. Performance cited much more data that described the school program than did Mr. Result.

   Mr. Resuls is concerned about low science achievement in the upper grades. Mr. Performance is concerned about inadequate staffing. Are they talking about the same concern? Both are obviously concerned with a limited school program, but the two evaluators' approaches obscure any direct comparison.

   Mr. Results is concerned about the negative impressions that are likely to occur from Mr. Swenson's ignoring criticisms. Mr. Performance is concerned that Mr. Swenson holds people at a distance and fails to use adequate feedback information and then make necessary program changes. The evaluators appear to share a common concern, but they use different data; Mr. Results listed "Critics Complaints" as useful data, and Mr. Performance made no mention of this data. Instead, he said that Mr. Swenson takes criticism in stride. Mr. Results does not seem to care how much distance Mr. Swenson keeps between himself and others—Mr. Results just expects Mr. Swenson to deal with criticisms.

   Mr. Results is concerned about the community impression that the school operates with "tight funds." It isn't true, and he says, "Swenson should correct this impression." Mr. Performance said nothing about the impression of "tight funds," but he did say, "the school has money," and he clearly implied that Mr. Swenson should spend some of it on Physical Education equipment. Both evaluators dealt with the school's finances, but in different ways. Both cited the need for Physical Education equipment as an important datum.

Mr. Performance called specific attention to a computer lab that is used almost as a toy by whoever wants to use it. He didn't say that, but his concern is clear. Mr. Results made no mention of this; maybe he doesn't like computers, but more likely, he didn't consider this datum relevant to this evaluation, because he chose to ignore it.

On the positive side, both evaluators found the students' and staff's hard work commendable. Both evaluators were impressed with the high level of community support and understanding of the school's academic goals. Both evaluators commended the school's safety record.

Mr. Performance found Mr. Swenson temperamentally well suited to work in the remote location, far from the normal amenities of civilization. (It's hard to ignore that this is a back-handed compliment.) This evaluator also congratulated Mr. Swenson for providing regular in-service education to his staff. He did not say anything about the specifics of the in-service in his written report, leaving a Third Party to ponder the substance of the comment. However, most managers will recognize that providing regular in-service programs does seem to warrant a compliment. Regardless of the in-service content or quality, paying attention to staff needs typically has a positive effect on workers performance. By definition, superior programs are better than poor programs.

PE Task 15: Comparing Readers' Findings and Judgments with the Two Examples

Having read the comparison between the "results" evaluation and the "performance" evaluation, readers should make their own additions to the items in the comparison. There may be factors to compare which were overlooked in the previous discussion. Readers may have developed an approach to evaluating Mr. Swenson which is quite different from the examples in this book, and may have focused on different criteria and used different data.

DO PE TASK 15 NOW

Readers should record any comparisons which have not been mentioned.

PE Task 16: Comparing the Evaluators' Recommendations for Action

Are the similarities between the two evaluations surprising? Probably not. After all, it was the same principal in the same school, and the evaluators had access to the same data which they each compared to a generalized concept of an ideal middle class U.S. school. If the readers' own evaluations are substantially at variance with these, the situation undoubtedly stems from a very different concept of the essence of an ideal school.

The fundamental difference between these two evaluations is found in the "first assumption" which each evaluator made, whether he believed it is correct to evaluate "results" or to evaluate "performance." Neither evaluator believed one evaluation system can logically hold principals accountable for school outcomes and administrative procedures simultaneously, even though there are principal evaluation systems that claim to do both, and (on the surface) appear to do so.

The difference between the basic starting points of the two evaluators did not keep them from having some common concerns for the case study school and its principal, Mr. Swenson. One common concern raised by both Mr. Results and Mr. Performance was a religious imbalance among the permanent staff and the possibility of this leading to the mis-education of the students and the creation of a poor school image.

Each evaluator reacted to this concern in a way consistent with his basic point of view. Mr. Results said, "Correct this," and offered no suggestions. Mr. Performance said, "Improve your staffing skills and your staffing pattern."

Mr. Performance has, in fact, accepted responsibility for the outcome if Mr. Swenson follows the directive of improving his staffing skills and his staffing pattern. Acting on that specific directive, Mr. Swenson is accountable for following the directive, not the result produced from following the directive. Should the parents' concern for religious indoctrination become a serious issue, Mr. Swenson can always say, "I did what my evaluator told me to do."

For his part, Mr. Performance will have to make sure that Mr. Swenson did, indeed, do what he was directed to do; if not, Mr. Performance may have to get a new principal. If Mr. Swenson truly follows the directive, and the situation still is not improved, then Mr. Performance must develop a new procedure for Mr. Swenson to follow.

Mr. Results isn't sure that any change in staff will produce the desired result; Mr. Results isn't there all the time. The principal is. And the principal has the authority to do whatever is necessary to bring about the desired change. Mr. Swenson may try five things without eliminating a concern for religious mis-education of students and say, "I have tried everything I can think of, and the problem's still here." Mr. Results will probably tell him what he told him the first time. And even if Mr. Results offers Mr. Swenson a suggestion for solving the problem, the advice Mr. Results offers is not a directive. Mr. Results will not excuse Mr. Swenson for creating a problem and then not accepting responsibility for the problem's solution. Mr. Results will go on telling Mr. Swenson to solve the problem (to produce a desired outcome) until the problem is solved or until the government decides to get another principal to replace Mr. Swenson.

An evaluator who attempts to combine the two approaches must continuously decide whether each of his directives is truly a directive or merely a suggestion. Evaluators can offer suggestions and still hold principals accountable for outcomes, because principals are free to ignore suggestions and act according to their own (the principals') best judgments. But the evaluator is accountable for the outcomes that result when principals do follow his (the evaluator's) directives.

Both Mr. Results and Mr. Performance have recommended that the government should "grant no further tuition increases until the deficiencies are corrected."

Mr. Results wants to revise the contract to include bi-annual financial audits. Mr. Performance wants the principal evaluated annually.

DO PE TASK 16 NOW

Readers should record further recommendations for action.

PE Task 17: Choosing the Best Approach for Principals

Readers should consider which system accorded Mr. Swenson the greatest respect. That is an important consideration, because at the center of every personnel evaluation is a person with feelings, talents, and fears. Personnel evaluations are not very good if that basic point is forgotten.

DO PE TASK 17 NOW

Readers should write down their opinions regarding which principal evaluation system, the results-based approach or the performance-based approach, demonstrated superior consideration for Mr. Swenson, as both a school principal and as a human being. Readers are urged to write an additional statement to support whichever choice they made.

PE Task 18: Choosing the Best Approach for Students

Readers should decide which approach to principal evaluation, results-based or performance-based, will most likely benefit the students of The International School.

DO PE TASK 18 NOW

Readers should record a choice and the rationale for having made it.

In Summary

The following are some of the important tasks readers have now completed in PE Tasks 1 through 18. These will provide a basis for readers to design their own principal evaluation systems.

1. PE Task 1 produced a description of what the reader expects to find in a good school, which became the list of "good school standards."
2. PE Task 2 produced a general description of the readers' perception of principal accountability, which was rewritten as an accountability "concept statement."
3. In PE Task 3 the concept statement was analyzed in terms of its components, and this became the "criteria" list.
4. PE Task 4 did not require readers to write definitions of their criteria. Readers did learn that the definitions must include a statement of what is to be evaluated and a statement of expectations. Readers were to have written some examples and were told that they will return to this topic later in PE Task 20.
5. PE Task 5 did not require readers to identify the data they would need for use in their own evaluation systems, because the data was already provided in the case study example. But, readers did learn that data identification is something which must be done within their own evaluation systems. They were to have listed the types of data necessary for making a principal evaluation. Readers were told that they will return to this task later in PE Task 21.
6. In PE Task 6 readers learned that they must specify the methods they will use in gathering data. Readers did not have to specify their data gathering methods to complete the case study evaluation, because the case study data was provided. Readers were to find out and record which of the evaluation system types is currently being used in their school systems, to write a brief list of its expectations, to decide whether or not they were "fair," and to record the job title(s) of the person(s) who review principal evaluations in their school systems.
7. In PE Task 7 readers compared their own standards for a good school with the standards in the case study school.

8. In PE Task 8 readers examined the case study data and selected the data which was useful for their purposes.
9. In PE Task 9 readers ranked the importance of the data items they selected from the case study data.
10. In PE Task 10 readers grouped the case study data they had selected according to the evaluative criteria in PE Task 3.
11. In PE Task 11 readers compared their prioritized data from PE Task 10 with their criteria from PE Task 3 and recorded their findings and judgments.
12. In PE Task 12 readers recommended actions to be taken with the case study principal.
13. In PE Task 13 readers compared the data they used in the case study with the two sample evaluations.
14. In PE Task 14 readers compared the findings and judgments made in the two case study examples.
15. In PE Task 15 readers compared their own case study findings and judgments with the two examples.
16. In PE Task 16 readers compared the two case study example evaluations and further compared them with their own recommendations for action. Readers were able to see which approach, either "results-based" evaluation or "performance-based" evaluation, was most compatible with their beliefs.
17. In PE Task 17 readers made a decision concerning which approach to principal evaluation is most respectful of principals.
18. In PE Task 18 readers made a decision concerning which approach to principal evaluation is most likely to benefit students.

Having completed PE Tasks 1 through 18, readers have determined the basic nature of a principal evaluation system that will suit them. The readers' detailed written work describes their personal rationales for principal evaluation systems, for use in influencing the opinions of others in constructing principal evaluation systems.

7

Making the Principal Evaluation System Manageable

If a well-managed system is a system that works, then it is also a system that does what it is supposed to do and does it efficiently. It is:

> **well-planned** > **well-organized**
> **well-supervised** > **well-controlled**

[NOTE: **This chapter examines each of these four systems management functions, provides a definition for each term, and demonstrates how each function applies to principal evaluation systems. As readers cover each management function, they will be directed to complete additional portions of their own principal evaluation systems.]**

Planning the Principal Evaluation System

The "art of management" is the use of means to accomplish an end. "Planning" is a matter of identifying and then selecting from alternative choices; it is an essential management activity.

The first planning tasks are to determine what the ends are, put them into clear language, and then communicate them to the people who must cooperate and work to achieve them.

PE Task 2 in Chapter Three asked readers to write out a description of those areas for which principals are accountable. Also in Chapter Three it was stated that "The first purpose of principal evaluation is to make schools better, but there are other purposes." That statement has been made several times in this book.

However, until now, readers have not been asked to consider those other purposes or to state their own reasons for evaluating principals.

PE Task 19: Purposes for Principal Evaluation

The following is a list of purposes that superintendents offer as reasons for making evalu ations. Their responses convey various motivations. Some are more substantial than others. They are presented in no particular order.

1. The law requires it.
2. My School Board wants it.
3. Nobody requires it, but it is always talked about as such a good idea that I want to look good to my peers and my Board and the other people I'm trying to impress.
4. It gives me power:

   I can build a case to fire those who should be fired—I focus people's work on my priorities—I protect myself—I remind them who is boss.
5. It helps me to know my principals better and to support them.
6. It helps me to protect principals from unscrupulous board members and other political figures who would dismiss them unfairly.
7. It helps to coordinate the work of other district level managers so that they are all working on the same priorities in a given school.
8. It forces me to do an unpleasant task that I would probably otherwise avoid.

9. It's only fair, because principals have to evaluate teachers, and this way it looks like what's good for the goose is good for the gander.
10. Research has demonstrated that it is good for morale.
11. It keeps me in touch with what is going on.
12. It clarifies matters for the principals; they know what is wanted and expected.
13. It forces me to think out what I want and expect from each principal.
14. It is a portion of my way of holding myself accountable.
15. It is essential to keeping the organization focused on organization goals.
16. It helps us decide whom to promote.
17. It is the basis for giving merit bonuses.
18. Principals expect to be evaluated.
19. It happens anyway; a system only organizes it.
20. It brings goals into focus.
21. It brings principals' needs into focus.
22. It makes me feel like I've done my job.
23. It is something I enjoy doing.
24. It is a part of good public relations.
25. It causes principals to do a better job of evaluating their teachers.
26. It demonstrates to principals how personnel evaluation should be done.
27. It helps district management to decide on the principals' needs for staff.
28. It makes district management more effective in working with principals.
29. It helps to build the school board's confidence in the principals.
30. The teachers like it.
31. It helps to keep the edge between the teachers' demands for principal loyalty and the superintendent's need for principal loyalty.
32. It is critical for maintaining top level management's control of the system.

33. It is a part of making the system better for students.
34. The merits of personnel evaluation are so well demonstrated that it does not require any further justification.

Any of these statements can be the "end" to which a principal evaluation system aspires. A principal evaluation system can be designed and managed to accomplish any of these ends if the statement is expressed as a "purpose" of the system. However, many of these statements are unsuitable as purposes. How long would it be reasonable to expect a principal evaluation system to survive if its central purpose was to mislead the staff and public about principal competence where incompetence abounded?

In any case, school districts do have management needs which require an on-going principal evaluation system:

1. Management decides which principals will be promoted, retained, recognized, rewarded, assisted, censured or terminated. Management needs data to make these decisions, and the evaluation system provides this data.
2. Trustees and district-level administrators have a responsibility to be involved in the management of administrative personnel, and principal evaluation is an appropriate vehicle for meeting this need.
3. District resources and services should be used effectively throughout the district, and principal evaluation is a method of controlling the school systems' need to have resources and services used properly.

There are a number of reasons "why" superintendents evaluate principals. Some are "little" reasons (not necessarily unimportant), and others are "petty" reasons. A few are really "big" reasons, because they seem valid to almost everyone. They have what Carl Jung called "moral leverage," and the superintendent's greatest moral leverage for carrying out the principal evaluation system is the promise it holds for making schools better.

Planning for Your Needs in a Principal Evaluation System

It is important for readers to know "why" they are going to evaluate principals. Because "why it is being done" shapes the character of what is to be done and how it is to be done.

Before evaluating others, evaluators should know themselves and be able to recognize any personal vulnerabilities they might have which could influence their evaluations. Evaluators should ask themselves:

(a) Am I a good person?
(b) Am I honest?
(c) Do I care about the people I work with?
(d) Do petty emotions motivate me sometimes?
(e) Do I ever act with insufficient data?
(f) Do frustrations ever cloud my judgment?
(g) Do I face up to my own shortcomings?
(h) Do I ever want to get even?
(i) Is anger ever my motivator?

The truthful answer to each of these questions is "yes," because these things are true about everyone, and everyone knows they're true. The point is that successful evaluators recognize their weak as well as their strong features; and taking them into account, go ahead to conduct fair and exemplary personnel evaluations.

In a well managed school system, people now what they are doing when they evaluate personnel and why they are doing it.

DO PE TASK 19 NOW

Readers should finish this statement: "I want to evaluate principals because..." Write down the "public" reason or reasons. (Public reasons are the ones to be shared with anyone.)

Readers should then write their private reasons for wanting to evaluate principals, the ones that only benefit readers.

Planning the Evaluation Data

PE Task 20: Written Criteria Definitions

Readers identified their standards for a good school in Chapter Three and named their criteria for judging the principal's work. However, readers were not asked to define their criteria at that time. Now is the time to do so. (To review this topic, readers should see the criteria examples in Chapters Four and Five and their PE Task worksheets.)

Remember, each criterion definition must contain a statement of what is to be expected from the principal. Results-based evaluations specify standards as prescribed outcomes, and performance-based evaluations specify standards as performance objectives. (Appendix B and Appendix C list examples of each type.)

DO PE TASK 20 NOW

Readers should write definitions for each criterion in their principal evaluation systems.

PE Task 21: Constructing the Data List

In Chapter Three readers were not asked to list the data that they would use in their own principal evaluation systems, because it was provided in the case study example. Now readers must specify the data that will be used in their principal evaluation systems. The data is the basis of the evaluation, and readers have to know what data they are going to use. Later, in PE Tasks 23 and 24, readers will be asked to develop roles and to assign personnel to carry out their principal evaluation systems. Knowing which data will be used for evaluating principals will influence those decisions.

Superintendents have a lot of data available for making evaluations of principals. With so much data, from so many sources, there is need for a way to classify it all. The following is a model for classifying principal evaluation data according to its source:

1. Data from documents:
   - 1.1 Produced by the principal while working
   - 1.2 Produced by others in relation to the school
   - 1.3 Produced as part of district operations
2. Data from direct observation:
   - 2.1 Staff meetings
   - 2.2 Teacher conferences
   - 2.3 PTA meetings
   - 2.4 School grounds
   - 2.5 Teachers at work
   - 2.6 Principals' meetings
   - 2.7 Extracurricular community events
3. Data from questioning:
   - 3.1 During planning sessions
   - 3.2 During sessions with a planned topic

3.3 During informal contacts

4. Data from hearsay:
   4.1 Informal communications from staff
   4.2 Informal communication from parents
   4.3 From developed questions asked of parents
   4.4 From developed questions asked of staff
5. Data from other sources of which readers may know

DO PE TASK 21 NOW

Readers should now make their own data source list with specifics identified.

Planning Materials

PE Task 22: Listing and Describing Forms

Evaluations should be written according to a standard form. What kind of "form" does the reader want to use? "Checklist" forms are used extensively, and those readers who like them will choose to develop their own. Because many different checklists are available, it isn't difficult to collect a wide assortment of them. The greatest limitation of checklists is that most are inflexible. The individual thoughts and words of the users/evaluators are subordinated to the words and concepts on the checklist.

Principals should be evaluated on every adopted criterion during each evaluation cycle (the time period and frequency during which evaluations are conducted). All principals are responsible for performing their jobs according to school system standards. Even though principals should be working toward specific objectives, no principal is absolved of the responsibility of running a safe and sane school. Every year, every school will encounter at least one unforeseen crisis. It is the principal's responsibility to see that the problem is handled and resolved.

Principals are entitled to know the level of "outcome" or "performance" for which they will be held accountable within each criterion. This information should be communicated in writing to each principal as the evaluation cycle begins and be further reflected in each final written evaluation.

The least complex printed evaluation form will include a minimum of printed headings: names, dates, criterion headings, and spaces for listing annual performance objectives and standards.

A blank sheet of paper can be a form, but the evaluator should follow a standardized, system-adopted format when writing individual principal reports and evaluations. A standardized format specifies the topics that will be covered and the order in which they will be presented.

The following is one example of an uncomplicated principal evaluation checklist form. It is not presented as a recommended model, only as an example that is actually used.

A Principal's Performance Evaluation Checklist

1—Outstanding: Exceeds requirements; 2—Acceptable: Meets requirements; 3—Unacceptable: Does not meet requirements

	Descriptive Item	Rating
1.	Demonstrates leadership	
2.	Provides clear direction	
3.	Is resourceful	
4.	Anticipates problems	
5.	Has good rapport with faculty	
6.	Maintains rich school environment	
7.	Supervises even-handedly	
8.	Observes teachers	
9.	Lessens teachers' non-teaching duties	
10.	Promotes respect among staff	
11.	Serves instructional goals	
12.	Supports teachers	
13.	Shows more concern with education than with appearances	
14.	Encourages teacher initiative	
15.	Conducts meaningful faculty meetings	
16.	Establishes efficient schedules	
17.	Welcomes criticism	
18.	Understands complex ideas	
19.	Displays emotional maturity	
20.	Makes books, supplies easily available	
21.	Fosters high faculty morale	
22.	Avoids militaristic atmosphere	
23.	Promotes harmony	
24.	Settles grievances fairly	
25.	Respects teacher rights	
26.	Sets realistic student discipline standards	
27.	Promotes community cooperation	
29.	Reprimands teachers only for just cause	
30.	Spends school funds in best interest of instruction	
31.	Exercises administrative discretion	
32.	Is firm, not domineering	
33.	Does not vacillate	
34.	Involves faculty in setting school policy	
35.	Respected by teachers	
36.	Respected by students	
37.	Respected by parents and community	

Here is another example of a checklist form. It is not presented as a recommended model, only as an example that is actually used.

Principal Evaluation Checklist #2

Name____

School______________________ Date________________

Ratings: O - Outstanding; S - Satisfactory; U - Unacceptable

	Item	Rating
1.	**Management Skills:**	
	Planning	
	Loyalty to School System	
	Team Player	
	Follows Lines of Authority	
	Evaluates Subordinates	
2.	**Instructional Leadership:**	
	Supervises According to School System Program	
	Employs Sound Principles of Learning	
	Assists Teachers	
	Demonstrates Ability to Work with Unsatisfactory Performance in Teachers	
3.	**Curriculum:**	
	Develops School Plans According to School System Guidelines	
	Monitors Student Progress	
	Protects Instructional Time	
	Sets High Standards and Expectations	
4.	**School Climate:**	
	Displays skills in Human Relations	
	Establishes Atmosphere of Trust in School	
	Motivates Students and Staff	
	Involves Staff and Parents in Decision-Making	
	Establishes an Orderly Environment	

Evaluator's Comments and Signature

Principal's Signature

Whatever form is selected, the evaluators' final judgment about the quality of the principal's work must be clear to the third party reader. Many forms contain a series of "check boxes" where evaluators must check off their final assessments:

Outstanding_____ Acceptable_____ Unacceptable_____

DO PE TASK 22 NOW

Readers should list the forms they will use in their preferred principal evaluation systems, and describe or sketch each form.

Organizing the Principal Evaluation System: Developing and Assigning Roles

Organizing systems is a management activity that formulates intentions and structures roles. Organizing an event grows from the need to have people cooperate and work in a coordinated fashion. Systems do not manage themselves; people manage systems.

Roles are not the same thing as positions: a person in the position of actor plays a role in a theater, a person in the position of teacher plays an instructional role in a school. Role descriptions tell us what an actor will do in the play or what a teacher will do in a school.

Roles are defined and described, then people fill them. For example, if evaluators want data that describe student achievement, obviously, the students will be the source of this data (at least some of the students). Someone has to elicit the data from the students. The role of that someone describes what is to be done, i.e., "construct and/or purchase student achievement tests, administer the student testing program, and forward the data to the principal's evaluator." If there is already a testing program in operation, this role can be executed by one person or in parts by several people.

PE Task 23: Developing Roles

In order to develop role descriptions for use in a principal evaluation system, the first step is to describe and name every job that has anything to do with the job of principal.

Principals, superintendents and trustees will be involved in the principal evaluation system. In any new plan, they will probably have new responsibilities which must be carefully described and determined beforehand. With that small caveat, readers should develop answers for the following:

1. Since the superintendent will perform the principals' evaluator role (unless this responsibility is delegated to someone else), what is the superintendent's role definition to be in the principal evaluation system? (**Example:** The superintendent evaluates all principals; he is responsible for setting annual performance objectives for each principal and for carrying out the adopted principal evaluation system.)
2. The principals will be evaluatees. What other roles and activities do they perform? (**Example:** The principals' role requires them to suggest their own personal objectives for the evaluator to use in the evaluation.)
3. School boards typically must act on, or ratify, all personnel actions. What is the role definition of the school board in carrying out the principal evaluation system? (**Example:** members of the Board of Education will annually: adopt district goals and objectives, review all principal evaluations, review the superintendent's recommended actions, and take whatever action they deem appropriate.)
4. Will the evaluators do every step required to carry out the evaluations, or will they have assistance; and if so, who will help and in which

ways? Will evaluators identify all the data and gather it themselves, or will these tasks be assigned to others? If the tasks are assigned, then describe the alternative roles for data gathering. (**Example:** the roles of assistant superintendents and other district level administrators require them to provide the superintendent with the principal evaluation data he or she requests.)

DO PE TASK 23 NOW

Readers should now write he role statements required in their principal evaluation systems.

PE Task 24: Assigning Roles

Example role definitions for superintendents, principals, and trustees were described in PE Task 23. It is now appropriate to "staff" the roles that readers have identified in their principal evaluation systems. Readers must choose the people who will perform the roles.

Readers should now choose the people to fill these and other roles that they developed in their individual principal evaluation systems. There can be some overlapping. More than one person can gather test data, for example, but pursuing identical assignments should be avoided. The Physical Education director supplies physical fitness test data, the curriculum director supplies reading scores, and the assistant superintendent for Education coordinates their efforts. Which of these positions should supply the evaluator with these data? Will one person coordinate the data collection and forward all data to the evaluator, or will each person individually forward the data he or she has been responsible for collecting?

More than likely, readers will want some data from a particular person, and they won't want other people having access to (messing around with) it. Readers will want to directly assign the work of data collecting in order to get the most efficient results.

DO PE TASK 24 NOW

Readers should use the role statements they developed in PE Task 23 to complete this task. Alongside each role statement, readers should record the job title of the person responsible for carrying out each role.

Organizing Time

PE Task 25: Constructing Time-Lines

Each cycle in a personnel evaluation system includes a series of events that are conducted according to prescribed procedures and executed by designated people at precise times. The following is an example of events that are listed on a principal evaluation system time-line:

July 10:	Assistant superintendent of Education submits to superintendent a report on school and district accomplishments from the previous year.
July 14:	Superintendent meets with board to review last year's results and set goals for the year.
July 15-31:	Superintendent prepares preliminary objectives for principal evaluations.
Aug. 1-15:	Superintendent reviews preliminary objectives with assistant superintendents.

Aug. 1-15:	Assistant superintendent of Business reviews individual school budgets with the superintendent.
Aug. 16-30:	Superintendent meets with each principal to review principal's suggested objectives.
Aug. 31:	Superintendent meets with board to establish annual objectives.
Aug. 31:	Board adopts annual objectives.
Sept. 1-15:	Principals receive annual objectives from the superintendent.
Oct. 1:	Assistant superintendent of Education submits fall testing results to superintendent.
Oct. 2-15:	Superintendent meets with each principal to make necessary adjustment in objectives.
Jan. 2-4:	Superintendent and assistant superintendents meet to review status of district progress.
Jan. 5-15:	Superintendent—principal midyear evaluation conferences are held to review progress the principal is making toward achieving his objectives and to make any appropriate changes in the evaluation plan.
March 1:	Preliminary notices of deficiency sent to appropriate principals.
May 15:	Assistant superintendent of Education submits spring test results to superintendent.
June 1:	Assistant superintendent of Business reviews all school budgets with superintendent.
June 2-15:	Superintendent holds year-end evaluation conferences with individual principals.
June 15-20:	Superintendent prepares final written principal evaluations.

June 21:	Board reviews all written principal evaluations and takes actions.
June 22-29:	Superintendent meets with each principal and reports board actions.
After June 29:	Principals have the opportunity to meet and discuss their disagreements with the school board's actions.

The purpose of the time-line is to insure that everything that needs to be done in carrying out the principal evaluation system is communicated to the responsible parties, and everything that needs to be done gets done. Principals are obviously the key figures in the process. They have the most to gain or lose. They want to know exactly how and when the principal evaluation system will affect them.

The following statements are presented to readers as factors to keep in mind as they construct their own time-lines.

1. The cycle begins for the principal when he or she finds out the specifics of his/her accountability during the current evaluation cycle. An evaluator-principal conference is a good method for informing the principal about this, but the evaluator could just send a letter telling the principal the specifics for which he or she is to be held accountable.
2. Data must arrive in a timely manner where it is needed. Some data will arrive according to predetermined schedules, in which case the evaluation events must be adjusted to fit these schedules. Also, all the data will not arrive at the same time, but that shouldn't be a problem. Careful scheduling will make sure that the evaluator will have what is needed, when it is needed.
3. The principal is entitled to know if the evaluator has discovered or suspects any deficiency early enough to make the necessary corrections. The cycle must provide for a written

notification of such things and a reasonable time for the principal to respond.

4. The evaluator should confer with the principal about his findings and judgments before preparing the written evaluation. This is not only fair, it helps clarify misperceptions and prepares the principal for the final written evaluation.
5. The written evaluation should be completed in time to allow the school board to take the recommended action.
6. Evaluators may want to include more meetings with the principal than are outlined here, and they may want to meet regularly with other members of their staff regarding principal evaluations; if so, include these events in the evaluation cycle schedule.
7. The principal evaluation system may include more written reports than are mentioned here; if so, provide time for the reports to be written and delivered.

DO PE TASK 25 NOW

Readers should now prepare a time-line of the events in their principal evaluation systems.

Supervising the Principal Evaluation System

Supervision is a management function dealing with directing the work of employees. Some workers are closely supervised and others receive little or no direct supervision. Principals work under loose supervision. Most school administrators work under loose supervision. Therefore, the effective strategy for keeping their work properly directed is appropriate initial training, followed by prudent application of effective control mechanisms.

PE Task 26: Training Personnel to Carry out the Principal Evaluation System

Readers created role descriptions for their principal evaluation systems and then assigned personnel, by job designations, to those roles. The next task is to decide if the personnel will need training. Don't overlook the evaluators—they may need training to fulfill their responsibilities. The following are typical training needs:

1. Principals will attend a district sponsored workshop on preparing objectives.
2. Superintendent and board members will attend a National School Board Association workshop on rewarding principals for good work.
3. Assistant superintendents will read a Harvard Business School publication on preparing effective reports for superiors.
4. Board members and administrators will attend a two-day symposium on the newly adopted principal evaluation system.

DO PE TASK 26 NOW

Readers should now list the training needs of each position and note the suitable training programs for use in meeting these needs.

PE Task 27: Controlling the Principal Evaluation System

Controlling is a management function that measures and corrects performance to ensure that objectives are accomplished and plans are fulfilled. Obviously, "personnel evaluation" is itself a controlling activity, because it measures and corrects performance. There must be standards in order to control effectively, otherwise controlling efforts become erratic and inconsistent.

Readers described the roles required to execute the elements in their principal evaluation systems. They expect role players to perform their responsibilities exactly as described and at the proper time. To insure this, evaluators must maintain some kind of record keeping system that logs the events and activities as they are completed, and also that reminds evaluators when scheduled items are not completed. One relatively simple method of maintaining such a log is to develop an annual management calendar which lists all such events.

The time-line prepared earlier specified events and actions that are part of the readers' principal evaluation systems. The next step is to specify what the evaluator will do to assess that each has been completed and to maintain an accurate record.

The performance standard for many of these events is merely that the required data arrives on time in the specified form. (Example: each school's achievement test data covers pages of numbers, but the evaluator receives a one page summary for each school from the school system test coordinator.) Other requirements may be written reports submitted to the evaluator, and the standard requirement would be that they should include specific topics following a specific format. (Example: the assistant superintendent's written report on the principals' effective use of district resources.) And still other events may produce no paper at all, in which case a checklist can be developed to record the events' occurrence. (Example: meetings with trustees that involve principal evaluation.)

DO PE TASK 27 NOW

Readers should now write out their lists of schedule controls for their principal evaluation systems.

8

Making the Principal Evaluation System Understandable and Supportable

This chapter covers the aspects of the principal evaluation system which will serve to bring it into precise focus on the conditions in a particular school system.

The principal evaluation system should enlist the support and involvement of its participants; it should be directed toward job improvement and personal growth; it must be adaptable to accommodate variations in individual principals; it should effectively incorporate the annual goals and objectives of the district; and it should be responsive to unexpected problems.

Making the Principal Evaluation System Understandable

The principal evaluation system must be understandable if it is to survive. It will be understood if it is clearly explained, and if people make an effort to understand it. Motivating them to make that effort is an important consideration.

A personnel evaluation system must satisfy some need, or needs, of the parties it serves if it is to survive. School board members will participate in the principal evaluation system, because their participation contributes to meeting their responsibilities as district policy makers and public overseers. Trustees of all independent schools or school systems are involved in principal evaluations, whether there is a formal principal evaluation system or not; whether they have specified roles in principal evaluation or not. The trustees' primary responsibilities deal with fundamental school management decisions.

Superintendents require their boards to act according to policy rather than individual whim. Superintendents endorse having a principal evaluation system in place, because they work best when they have good policy guidance. Likewise, good personnel policy delimits and controls meddling.

Principals will want to be (and must be) involved in the design and implementation of a principal evaluation system, because their professional "fates" are determined by its content. Also, they need to invest in the system in order to have confidence in its application.

PE Task 28: Techniques to Be Used with the School Board

Part of the reader/evaluator's job is to get school board members involved, to get them to "buy in" on the creation or upgrading of a principal evaluation system. Practically, this involves getting the school board to accept, support, and carry out their role(s) in the principal evaluation system. Some boards prefer formal structures and approaches, while others do virtually everything on an informal, ad hoc basis.

No one knows a school board's members as well as the superintendent whom they hired. And no one can tell a superintendent exactly how to get trustees involved in the workings of a principal evaluation system. Superintendents know (or have to find out) the techniques that will work with their schools' trustees. The board members themselves are the ones who will convey to their superintendent the methods they prefer and the methods they reject. They will inform the superintendent of their preferences, sometimes directly and other times through inference and foot dragging.

The success of the principal evaluation system is dependent upon the entire board's actions, and many individual trustees (and some school boards) are reluctant to take personnel actions of any kind, either positive or negative, which are directed toward a specific person. Yet, successful personnel evaluation systems lead ultimately to such actions which only the school board can decide to make. Trustees, after all, are elected local public officials. Common sense politics tells them that an individual under fire from a large organization is the underdog, and politicians are vulnerable when they attack an underdog. Conversely, public displays of political favoritism are also suspect. Most trustees (just as with other people) are more willing to take action, even unpleasant action, if they see the action linked with their own objectives. For their part, school board members are more likely to take action which is required by their own policies.

Readers should consider their own school systems and the trustees who govern them, and then decide on ways to effectively involve their school boards in developing principal evaluation systems. The objective is that in subsequent days, school board members will contribute to the success of the principal evaluation system that is finally adopted.

DO PE TASK 28 NOW

Readers should make a list of the techniques and strategies that can be used which will help to involve the readers' school board members in the principal evaluation system.

PE Task 29: Identifying Rewards for Principals

Most people prefer to act positively rather than negatively, and most board members would prefer to be "good guys" rather than "bad guys." The opportunity to effectively reward good work is also an opportunity to be a good guy. The principal evaluation system should lead to such rewards.

School districts often do not have many opportunities for advancement, but some opportunities do exist. Very few school districts pay merit bonuses for good work. Only a few do this, although many school districts are not prohibited from paying merit bonuses. Most school districts have some form of "personnel recognition" in operation, and some of these could be adapted to help meet the reward making needs of a principal evaluation system. A record for outstanding work can get principals advanced positions in larger school systems where more promotional opportunities exist. A good record can lead to recognition from professional associations and in some cases the receipt of special project and study grants.

DO PE TASK 29 NOW

Readers should identify and make a list of potential rewards that can be used in their school systems to recognize and reward the good work of principals.

PE Task 30: School Board Activities in a Principal Evaluation

School boards vary in their degrees of involvement in the operations of school systems. Some boards are satisfied to adopt goals and ratify staff recommendations, while others want an active ongoing role in evaluation. When a school board becomes too heavily involved in administrative detail work, it can be difficult to inform its members about implementing principal evaluation procedures. In most cases it is better to decide exactly what the board's involvement will be before implementing a new principal evaluation system.

Earlier, readers wrote out a role description for school boards in a principal evaluation system. Likewise, they developed a timeline for activities and events. Additionally, there may be some preferences for school board participation which are not contained in either of these. For example, readers may want the board members to visit each school once or twice a year. These visits are not for snooping purposes, but to give the board members a feeling for each campus.

DO PE TASK 30 NOW

Readers should make a list of the activities with which they want their school boards and individual members to become involved with in their principal evaluation systems.

[NOTE: Some readers may wish to make a second list of activities they want school board members to leave alone. Although in most school systems, board members become involved in whatever they choose. After all, they have the highest degree of public accountability of anyone associated with the school system. They stand for election, and their personal reputations are placed in cold public view. While everyone cares about his or her public reputation, few people in society take such serious risks with their good names as do school board members.]

Support from the Principals

PE Task 31: Principals' Fairness Issues

It is all but impossible for a principal to be disinterested in his own evaluation. Even so, principals can pretend to accept the process and simultaneously work for its failure, if they resent the intrusion of the evaluator or lack confidence in the principal evaluation system. If a principal is caught deliberately trying to undermine the evaluation system, he or she deserves to be fired. But reality often puts such things in a gray zone of uncertainty.

Superintendents have a legal and moral right to expect their principals to behave ethically. The administrative relationship is not the same as the usual relationship between an employee and an employer. Superintendents have a special fiduciary relationship (working together in a trustworthy manner) with their subordinate administrators that is a prerequisite to managing the school district. Courts have upheld the necessity of this concept to the special working relationship between a school superintendent and his subordinate managers.

People have deeply-rooted concepts of "fair play," and the principal evaluation system should honor these concepts by holding principals accountable in a fair way. (Courts have also upheld this concept on behalf of principals.) The data actually put into use in making evaluations are chosen arbitrarily by evaluators. Only they really know what they turn over in their minds while making their judgments. Evaluators do know that their judgments must withstand third party scrutiny. They must pass some litmus test of fairness. Principals should know and be comforted by this also.

How will evaluators judge a principal's performance when the conditions for effective work do not exist, and only those responsible for them (supervisors, superintendents, school boards, legislatures, and governors) can alter those conditions? The most competent principal is ineffective when circumstances are beyond his or her control. "Could he or she really have done anything about it?" "Was it beyond him or her?" The answers to these questions should be determined with fairness.

Principals name three things as the most persistent obstructions to their work. Principals have limited (or no) control over any of them. Yet, each effects their professional roles on a daily basis.

> *Collective Bargaining*

> *School System Management Practices and Policies*

> *Personal Style of System-Wide Administrators*

In addition to the school system's bargaining posture (combative or congenial), there are contract items that can and do severely limit principal decision making authority regarding staff assignments. There are many aspects of school system operation that can hamper principal effectiveness, such as:

> *Does the school system hire well-trained and experienced teachers, or does it hire less costly personnel?*

> *How much investment does the school system make in the continuing education of its staff?*

> *What kind of teacher is the school system able to attract and employ?*

Some school systems have greater skill recruiting the best talent. Salaries are a factor, but a school system's reputation is more important.

A principal's options for taking action are proscribed by law and school system policy. Those policies may be reasonable or unreasonable; they may be written confusedly or in plain, clearly understandable language.

Principals need a clear, operational understanding of what the school system will tolerate. They need an understanding of roles: their own, their subordinates, and the various authority figures with whom they deal. Surveys of principals have shown that "lack of clarity" is a common complaint.

Principals complain about interruptions and unpredictable demands. Routine management becomes cumbersome through poor timing, poor conceptualization, and poor coordination. Ambiguity and uncertainty are a way of life for administrators, but they administer more effectively in a clearly defined and stable management system.

How much professional autonomy is extended to principals? The "big boss" who is "the source of all new procedures and changes" restricts creative administration and inhibits administrative judgment. On the other extreme, the "don't bother me and I won't bother you" style extends too much autonomy. In some school systems, principals are perceived as independent managers—in others they are little more than clerks. Whichever management "style" or "tone" does exist, the school system's management is responsible for it. In any case, management style is a parameter within which principals must work, not something which they create. Principals are selected. They do not select the managers who work over them.

Virtually all organizations composed of principals agree that the factors listed above significantly impact their jobs. The factors were stated in negative terms, because it is their "negative aspects" that affect principals' notions of fair play.

These issues may be minor considerations in some school systems, or they may be major. (Readers are in the best position to judge their own situations.) Other issues that effect principals' concepts of fairness may not have been mentioned here. Readers are in the best position to know the issues and how they should be addressed in their school systems.

Evaluators themselves become the final determinants as to how much support the school board and the principals will give to the principal evaluation system. Once a new principal evaluation system begins to operate, the pattern of the evaluators' judgments will soon be evident to principals and board members. Evaluators must be watched carefully for their consistency (and adaptability to the unexpected) as they carry out their evaluations of principals. The evaluators' good judgment is the most important ingredient for making the principal evaluation system succeed.

DO PE TASK 31 NOW

Readers should make a list of the kinds of issues (and their particulars) that principals in their school systems will want resolved in order to come to regard the principal evaluation system as being fair.

PE Task 32: Evaluating the Effectiveness of the Principal Evaluation System

If the schools don't benefit, if the students' education is not improved, then why bother? There is no way to make a principal evaluation without causing the evaluator to experience stress. There is no way to enact a principal evaluation system without causing others to experience stress. Should evaluators and principals experience stress without a hope that the schools will get better? Of course not. And the good news is that schools do improve with effective leadership and the benefits of evaluation. The causes and results of the improvements are easily recognized, and principals are consistently named as significant contributors to the improvements.

As readers begin to put their new principal evaluation system into action, they should take a benchmark measure of where the schools stand at present, and then repeat that measurement each year. The "Standards for a Good School" listed in PE Task 1 are the areas to monitor. Each standard contains either an identified or an implied measurement factor. In some instances school systems will need to develop or adopt measurements for specific standards. (A basic process for doing this can be adapted from the activities suggested in this book.)

The changes that occur in measured student and school outcomes will not always be directly linked with leadership; as a matter of fact, it is sometimes impossible to make a direct connection. However, a pattern of growth or decline does reflect the effectiveness of school leadership.

The pattern of change does not always show up quickly. Sometimes it takes years to reverse a downward trend. At other times a new face arrives on the scene just as the good news starts to register in the findings. As a result, the credit can be misplaced with the newcomer. This is a sad event for those who actually worked long and hard to make things better. Often, their only satisfaction will come from knowing that they did the good work that led to better results. However, principals can (and should) be recognized for their good work in a timely manner, if they are a part of a good principal evaluation system.

DO PE TASK 32 NOW

Readers should make a list of the types of data they will use in the benchmark measurement of their school systems. Their findings will provide a standard against which to assess the improvement in their schools in future years.

[NOTE: There are many ways to involve people in a project, to gain their support for its goals, to reward good work, to deal with fairness problems and to evaluate schools. The particular methods chosen must match the situation, and when good methods are employed, good results ensue. Good results, in turn, have a utility of their own. Through their use, evaluators will sharpen and hone their evaluative skills which will lead to a more rational working environment for principals.]

9

Supervising Principals

Supervision is a management activity that deals with directing the work of subordinates. There is a distinction between employee supervision and employee evaluation.

Supervision includes:

1. Assigning work to subordinates;
2. Ratifying the plans of subordinates;
3. Assisting subordinates to achieve assigned objectives;
4. Monitoring the performance of subordinates;
5. Providing in-service training for subordinates; and
6. Judging the work performance quality of subordinates.

Each of these six items is an aspect of directing the work of employees. Each is a supervisory activity. Readers will recognize that in many school systems, the same individual who carries out these activities with principals is also the one who will evaluate those principals. However, the individual who directs the principal to do each of the above activities may not be the evaluator who judges the sufficiency of the principal's work performance and then prepares the formal principal evaluation.

A supervisor judges the quality of a subordinate's work performance as he directs it, but the supervisor may not be the employee's designated evaluator. The distinction between the role of the supervisor and the role of the evaluator is as follows:

> The evaluator is the individual with the specific responsibility to evaluate and prepare the final written evaluation. The evaluator could conceivably have no direct contact with the principal, relying completely on data about the principal, but collected by others. The evaluator may never need to offer a moment's help to the principal, or even to communicate agreement or disagreement with the principal's declared intentions. This is admittedly an extreme and unlikely situation, but it doesn't violate the basic tenets of the evaluator's role, which is to make judgments regarding the sufficiency of the principals.
>
> The supervisor directs the employee's actual work performance, gives directions, offers suggestions, provides help, and carries on some form of ongoing monitoring of the employee's work. The judgments the supervisor makes about the employee's work are to keep the worker on track, not for the purpose of giving a bonus, promotion, transfer, or dismissal.

The following example concerns a principal involved with both a supervisor and an evaluator. The supervisor reminds the principal to complete an overdue task (in the supervisor's judgment, the task was not completed within the required time standard, although he had directed the principal to get the task done). The supervisor informed the principal's evaluator about the delay. It is up to the evaluator to decide whether or not the principal's failure to do the task on time should become a part of the principal's evaluation report. The evaluator may not even bother to find out why the delay occurred (but he should). The supervisor is not in the position to make this a part of the principal's evaluation, because the supervisor is not the evaluator. The evaluator, and he alone, decides whether or not to include this factor in the principal's written evaluation report.

A supervisor is not an evaluator unless he or she is designated to be one and is assigned evaluation responsibilities in addition to supervisory responsibilities. An extreme example will demonstrate this point: A results-based evaluator can receive written reports from a principal's supervisor and all the other data necessary to use in evaluating a principal without seeing the supervisor, the principal, or the school; all the evaluator needs to complete the evaluation are the data and the evaluative criteria. That is to say, the evaluator can write an evaluation report about the principal, sight unseen. However, the sight unseen practice leaves too many loose ends. It just isn't a good idea.

Superintendents do not have to supervise principals at all, although failing to do so is poor practice. Principal supervision responsibilities can be assigned to one or more people, and the superintendents can do the evaluating themselves. Superintendents can delegate both the supervision responsibilities and the evaluation responsibilities to one person (such as an assistant superintendent who can be both principal supervisor and principal evaluator), or to two people who both report to the superintendent (such as the director of Elementary Education who supervises elementary principals and the assistant superintendent for Educational Services who evaluates elementary principals).

A traditional management concept suggests that one person be selected to perform both supervision and evaluation responsibilities (the "One man—One boss" axiom). Principals' real-life work may make this traditional concept difficult to follow in larger school systems where many different system level administrators head specific programs operating in each individual school.

The idea of one person, one boss is a shorthand description of the "Unity of Command" concept. This concept recognizes that employees with a single supervisor have fewer difficulties understanding instructions and have a greater feeling of personal responsibility for results than do employees with more than one immediate superior. The "Unity of Command" concept makes it easier to hold individuals accountable. Employees report to one individual and are accountable to that same individual.

A second traditional management concept called "Harmony of Objectives" deals with blending the organization's objectives with the personal objectives of an employee. The greater the compatibility between personal objectives and organizational objectives, the greater the productivity and job satisfaction of the employee.

Traditional management theory holds a third concept that the more effective the direction of employees, the greater their contribution will be in furthering the organizational goals. This concept is called "The Effect of Directed Objectives." It, too, deserves some consideration in the development of principal supervision plans.

These three concepts, "Unity of Command," "Harmony of Objectives" and "The Effect of Directed Objectives" are derived from extensive experience, and their validity is supported by a considerable amount of behavioral management research. These concepts, although not always followed perfectly, should be kept in mind.

Consider what the three management concepts mean to the principal in the following scenario. It is a list of hypothetical events that might occur within one week in the working life of a school principal.

Monday:

8:00 a.m. Director of Bilingual Education tells the principal that the latest test data show Hispanic students well below projected achievement objectives, and that the Hispanic students complain that they do not understand their teachers because the teachers only speak English. The Bilingual Director suggests the principal hire a consultant to teach the teachers basic classroom Spanish.

10:00 a.m. The director of Special Education tells the principal that Joey J. has reached the achievement level prescribed in his Individual Education Plan and should be returned to a regular classroom. The principal is told to arrange for the required meeting with staff and parents. The principal says that Joey's mother will not agree, but the director says the principal must see to it that Joey is returned to the regular program.

1:00 p.m. The director of the Instructional Materials Center informs the principal that a new Earth Science instruction kit is available for $500, and the science teachers need it to help meet their science objectives. He tells the principal that he should use school funds to buy it.

2:00 p.m. The assistant superintendent for Education visits the school and notices that the algebra textbook is different from the one used in other district schools. He tells the principal to get in line, and the principal says his math teachers consider the text used in his school to be superior to the district text.

Tuesday:

9:00 a.m. The principal arranges for a consultant to teach basic classroom Spanish to his faculty.

10:00 a.m. The principal orders the Earth Science kit. He discovers it costs $800, but he orders it anyway.

11:00 a.m. The principal makes arrangements for a Special Education meeting for Joey J.

1:00 p.m. The principal sends the faculty a bulletin saying that the regular staff meetings will be used for in-service education for the next five weeks to learn basic classroom Spanish.

3:30 p.m. Miss Dove, a Physical Education teacher, tells the principal that she intends to file a grievance for overtime pay for attending in-service training. The principal explains that the in-service will occur during regular working hours in accordance with the teachers' collective bargaining agreement.

3:40 p.m. Miss Dove files a formal labor grievance.

Wednesday:

9:00 a.m. The principal meets with the school's Bilingual Advisory Committee and tells them he has arranged for a consultant to teach basic classroom Spanish to teachers, so they will be better able to give directions and explanations to the students with limited English speaking abilities.

The committee chairperson objects and tells the principal to hire three more bilingual teacher aides with the money. A vote is taken, and the principal's plan is defeated seven to six. He tactfully reminds the committee that he appreciates their advice, but he must act according to his own best judgment. The committee agrees to send a letter of protest to the school board condemning the principal's arrogance. The vote is seven to six.

2:00 p.m. During the Special Education meeting, Joey J's mother says she does not want her boy placed back in the regular classroom program, and if Joey does not remain in the Special Education room, she will file for a "fair hearing." The principal explains all the reasons for Joey's return to the regular program, congratulates Joey, his mother, and the Special Education staff for the good work they have done, and reminds them that getting Joey into the "mainstream" is the objective of Special Education.

4:00 p.m. Mrs. J. calls the Parents Association for Handicapped Children and asks for their help at the fair hearing.

Thursday:

7:30 a.m. The assistant superintendent for Business Services calls the principal and cautions him that he is dangerously close to exceeding his Bilingual budget and his Instructional Materials budget.

9:00 a.m. The director of Personnel calls to say the teacher's union supports Miss Dove's grievance, and the principal may have to pay overtime to all his teachers out of his Bilingual funds. The principal says he doesn't have the money, and he acted within the contract's provisions. The director of Personnel says he has discussed the grievance with the school attorney, and the attorney feels that it might be a good idea to go ahead and pay the overtime.

Noon — The principal goes to a Rotary Club meeting and is kidded and fined five dollars for not standing up to the Hispanic pressure group.

Friday:

8:00 a.m. — The superintendent calls the principal and says he must talk to him. He invites the principal to lunch someplace where they can talk privately. The principal wonders who has gotten to his boss. He tries to shrug off the worry, but can't. After all, the superintendent is the person who evaluates him.

Noon — Over lunch the superintendent tells the principal he is the best school administrator in the district, never loses sight of what is good for the students, exercises good judgment, is not afraid of criticism, is willing to take a chance, is a very pleasant guy to be around, and he enjoys having lunch with him from time to time.

12:01 p.m. — The principal orders another round of sarsaparilla.

A superintendent of a small district, with three schools and no help other than a part-time business manager, would consider the last scenario ludicrous, and the only concern for "Unity of Command" is a struggle with a particular school board member who wants to act like he is the superintendent.

Most principals in North America work in large school systems with several layers of administrators, and each layer is trying to get each principal to do things its way.

Typically, a principal has many different people supervising his or her work, and that was the point of the example. The principal in the scenario was confronted by several system level administrators who supervise programs within the principal's school. The bilingual citizens committee oversees that program according to government guidelines. Individual parents, especially parents of handicapped children, have legal rights and due process procedures available to them to challenge school decisions regarding their students for no other reason than that they arbitrarily disagree. The critical question for the principal's evaluator is this: How much authority does each supervisor have to order the principal's behavior? The scenario principal listened to suggestions, then exercised his own judgment and accepted the consequences for his decisions. If a supervisor orders the principal to act in a particular way, taking away the principal's decision-making authority, then the supervisor is responsible for the outcomes of the decision, because the decision is the supervisor's, not the principal's. If the supervisor only suggests what the principal should do, the principal is not obligated to follow the suggestions. The principal is then accountable for the outcomes resulting from his or her decision.

In a results-based system, the principal is free to act according to his or her own judgment as long as that behavior stays within the district policy limits and its legal requirements. The supervisor may offer suggestions to the principal, but that's all.

Results-based systems extend principals' authority for decision-making beyond that of other principal evaluation systems. The principal's specific accountability is also apt to be stated more precisely than in other evaluation systems. To the extent that this is true, the supervisor and the principal both have a clear notion of what is expected of the principal, namely, to produce the desired results. The supervisor's job is no less challenging within this system than within another, but the real risk takers are the principals.

A performance-based principal evaluation system requires greater detailed specification of the supervisor's authority over principals, and the actual extent of the principals' authority to exercise their own independent judgments. The primary focus of a performance-based evaluation is the principal's administrative behavior. When in doubt, principals working under this type of evaluation system would do well to follow what supervisors recommend. In a performance-based evaluation system, administrative behavior can rate higher than results. The principals' accountability is linked to their performance objectives. The linkages are sometimes vague. "Staff morale" and "community support" are fuzzy things to measure. In any area where such ambiguity exists, the supervisor's job is effected, because he or she is responsible for helping principals meet their performance objectives.

Performance-based evaluation and supervision role assignments fit together neatly. The evaluator/supervisor and the principal work from a common understanding of the principal's expected performance with the fewest number of people involved, which should result in better communication and fewer misunderstandings. (It is easier to say than do, of course, because misunderstandings are facts of life. We are all misunderstood sometimes. As Emerson said, "To be great is to be misunderstood.")

The directions that principals' receive from their evaluators have "greater" potential consequences for the principals' professional well-being than what their supervisors might say. If principals receive conflicting messages from their evaluators and their supervisors, and they must choose to understand one or the other, the choice isn't difficult. In practice, the evaluator's directions are followed, while the supervisor's are ignored. This can make supervisors jobs difficult. They may become nothing more than impotent middle-men if the directions they give as supervisors are regularly ignored.

Principal supervisors who are not also principal evaluators must have a clear understanding of the extent of principal accountability. They need to understand that, as supervisors, some of their directions will be ignored by the principals whom they supervise.

Supervision: Comparing Close to Casual

Close supervision occurs on assembly lines where the supervisor is in attendance at all times. Virtually no practicing professional works under close supervision, certainly not teachers, and definitely not principals. Student professionals are often supervised closely, but once the "ticket" is earned, supervision practices change.

Casual supervision is both informal and occasional, and many educators do work under casual supervision. For the most part, principals work under a semi-casual form of supervision: they are observed and directed by the circumstances that bring their supervisors in touch with them. Those circumstances include:

(a) Direct contact with the principal according to a schedule; (For example: the supervisor will visit the principal's school once every month according to a printed school visitation calendar.)

(b) Contact with the principal resulting from something the principal has done that the supervisor wants to discuss;

(c) Incidental contact.

Pre-planning all the supervisor's school visits is too much like observing a "set performance," and when the supervisor has a need to see a preplanned event (perhaps a staff meeting), such events are appropriate for the supervisor to witness. But when he wants to see how it's "really going," he drops in, and the drop-in visit is a form of incidental contact.

Supervision is not the same thing as watching—supervision occurs when a subordinate is directed (ordered or advised) along a course of action, and when the supervisor is judging a subordinate's activities either directly or indirectly through the examination of some work product. Lots of people watch principals without supervising them. Even so, those people have no authority to direct what principals do. Principals always should be told who their supervisors are and the extent of each supervisor's authority.

Dividing the Principal's Responsibilities

Some school programs may be under the direct authority of a district administrator. In this case, the principal's responsibilities are not as great as they would be if the principal was in charge of the program. For example, Special Education programs are often the province of a Special Education administrator. The principal has a limited supervisory function and performs specific tasks within the school's Special Education programs. However, the principal does not have the authority to make final decisions or to modify the Special Education programs according to his or her own judgment. In such instances, the principal's normal responsibilities as the "administrator in charge" have been modified.

The Principal's Response to Supervision

Most principals do appreciate the help and support of a good supervisor, one with experience and sound judgment, just as they value a good evaluator, because through the assistance of good evaluation and supervision, they learn and grow better at their jobs.

Some principals want nothing to do with supervisors, perhaps from a lack of respect for the supervisor or because of the principal's personal vanity or fear. As Sophocles said, "To him who is in fear everything rustles." Everyone knows of a principal somewhere who is forever timid and afraid. The weakest principals need supervision the most and are often the most difficult to supervise.

This brief chapter is not intended to be a treatise on how to supervise principals. It does intend to make the distinction between supervision and evaluation. Further, it intends to demonstrate that supervising principals is an important activity and deserving of attention.

When constructing a principal evaluation system, principals and school boards will have many questions about principal supervision. If they have followed the same process that the reader has followed in developing his or her principal evaluation system, they will deal with supervision issues only after they have determined what the principal is accountable for and the process by which principals will be held accountable.

PE Task 33: Listing Principal Supervisors

The distinction between a supervisor and an evaluator is vitally important to principals' behavior. As was discussed earlier, a supervisor directs and an evaluator holds accountable. The evaluator has more authority for affecting principals' careers than do supervisors. Therefore, principals are ultimately accountable to their evaluators and must finally exercise their own best judgments in order to comply with their evaluators' expectations. Should the evaluator state, "Principals will follow all supervisor directives," then no confusion will exist. The real world of large school systems presents principals with numerous situations in which they must decide between what the supervisor directs and what the evaluator expects.

DO PE TASK 33 NOW

Readers should write a list of the supervisory positions (within their school systems) that are responsible for supervising principals. Also, place a check next to the following positions which have the responsibility for evaluating principals.

Supervisory Position	Supervision Responsibilities	Evaluates Principals *yes/no*
1. Superintendent	**District Level Administrators**	**x/**
2. Personnel Director	**District Personnel Programs**	**/x**
3. /		
4. /		

In this chapter supervision was identified as a management activity. A list was presented which identified supervisory activities. Three management concepts, "Unity of Command," "Harmony of Objectives," and "The Effect of Directed Objectives" were introduced and described. The differences between the roles of supervisor and evaluator and the different impacts each role has on principal behavior were discussed. The point was made that the roles of supervisor and evaluator can be combined within a single job position.

10

The Principal Job Description

PE Task 34: Writing the Principal Job Description

School systems typically have at least one job description for principals, and most state governments adopt their own versions as a part of their education regulations. It is entirely possible that the existing principal job descriptions are adequate for the needs of a new principal evaluation system. But the current job descriptions should be examined and compared with the new principal evaluation system, because job descriptions are an essential component of all principal evaluation systems.

Principal job descriptions are basic documents that describe the duties and responsibilities of school principals.

Job descriptions can be brief or lengthy. For example, California State Regulations specify:

- **5550. Principal**
  Local school boards shall assign a principal to each school.

- **5551. Administration of School**
  The principal is responsible for the supervision and administration of his or her school.

- **5552. Playground Supervision**
  Where playground supervision is not otherwise provided for, the principal will provide for supervision by certificated employees of the conduct and safety, and for the direction of play, of the pupils of the school who are on the school grounds during recess and other intermissions and before and after school.

- **5553. Dissemination of Information**
  The principal is responsible for disseminating information to students and staff regarding the legal requirements of students and staff members.

The State of California then goes on for thousands and thousands of pages to describe what the California schools will and will not do, who will do it, when it will be done, how it will be done, and the spirit in which it should be done. The combined Education Code and California Education Regulations are so voluminous that not a living soul knows all that is said in them.

Education law in most states resembles California's, although there are exceptions (the amount of state education law seems to be directly proportionate to the concept of state control versus local control of the schools). Further, this does not include the Federal laws on education; nor does it include the other laws governing fire and safety, building codes, criminal codes, juvenile justice codes, local ordinances, and the school district policy manual. All of these impinge on the principal's responsibilities.

The job description for the position of principal must synthesize this morass of legal requirements and delineate the principals' responsibilities so that principals know:

1. What they are responsible for;
2. What their duties are;
3. Where their authority lies;
4. Who their immediate superior is.

The tasks that readers have completed thus far have answered these four basic requirements for the principal job description. Readers need only review their work to construct a job description that contains all of these essential components.

The reason for making the principal job description include more than minimal requirements goes back to a point made several times in this book: "Written principal evaluations are subject to a Third Party review." When a Third Party reviews a principal evaluation to determine the sufficiency of that evaluation, the Third Party will, in most instances, compare the evaluation with the principal's role requirements as specified in the principal job description. It doesn't matter that all principal evaluations are not reviewed by a Third Party. It does matter that evaluations can be reviewed by a Third Party, and that the evaluator will want that Third Party to support his or her judgments.

School systems are expected to provide directions for their principals, and school system actions taken toward a principal will be judged by the clarity of the directions that were given to the principal. Certainly, any contradictions between the principal directions (or expectations) stated in one place (in the job description) and in another place (in the principal evaluation system manual) may become disadvantageous to the school system, just as any contradiction will be confusing to the principal.

Many school systems have "Management Handbooks" which describe the particulars of the work that managers must do in the school system, and how managers are expected to go about doing the work. Most school systems have adopted a school system philosophy statement which describes what the school system wants to do and sets a tone for the way people are to work. Making reference to these documents in the principal's job description may seem redundant. However, in a case of dispute in which the principal may challenge a ruling by his superior, the description will not appear redundant to a hearing officer. It may, in fact, prove the superior's point.

Courts have upheld superintendents' rights to expect loyalty from their subordinate administrators; not blind loyalty, of course, but honesty, candor and trust between superintendents and their administrators is a necessary condition. Superintendents probably will not experience the same high level of trust with other staff members, but they are correct to hold higher standards for administrators. Some reference to this topic is appropriate within the job descriptions for principals.

The job descriptions for principals may include the qualifications for each position. (Example: a masters degree, five years teaching experience, and an administrative certificate). Qualifications are especially important to include if local standards are higher than state standards, or if a school system's standards are higher than those in the neighboring school systems. Otherwise, a third party will assume that the prevailing standards apply. Unless standards are stated assumptions, misconceptions will abound.

School systems have laws and policies that govern the duration of principal contracts, the beginning and ending dates of principal contracts, and the procedures for notifying principals as to whether their contracts will be renewed or canceled. School system administrators may not want their policy book getting fatter by duplicating these things in the principals' job descriptions. However, they should include the policy numbers and code numbers as a part of the job descriptions. Such references are an additional step toward making full disclosure of the role of principals, their rights, and the school system's expectations. The decisions regarding which law and policy references to include and which to exclude are best made by the authorities in the local school system.

How Many Principal Job Descriptions Are Necessary?

All principals are accountable for some common expectations, and all principal job descriptions should be alike in regard to those identical expectations and duties. But elementary principals, middle school principals, junior high principals, high school principals, and special school principals do not have identical responsibilities. And all the principals in a district should not have identical job descriptions unless all their schools are of the same type. To answer the question of how many principal job descriptions are needed, readers only have to know how many different types of schools are in their school system and then write a principal job description for each different type of school.

This does not mean a different principal evaluation system is required for each group of principals (elementary, junior high, secondary and the like). It doesn't, because all the principal job descriptions are a part of the principal evaluation system. The job descriptions specify the duties and responsibilities of all principals within each principal group.

Readers are reminded of some particular tasks they have completed, PE Tasks 2, 3, 4, 5, 6, 20, and 21. During these tasks readers stated what principals are accountable for, the criteria for judging the performance of individual principals, the scope of the data evaluators will use in the evaluation, and how evaluators will gather that data. Completing those tasks establishes the basic elements of a uniform principal evaluation system, applicable to all principals working within particular school systems. Most importantly, the principal evaluation system adapts to the essence and needs of individual schools. Therefore, the pinpointed accountability of each principal is specifically related to improving the principal's performance (whether it is rated according to results or performance), thereby improving individual schools. This, after all, is what the principal evaluation system had to accomplish.

DO PE TASK 34 NOW

Readers should write principal job descriptions for their school systems.

A Concluding Note to Readers

Readers should congratulate themselves; they have worked hard and deserve to feel a genuine sense of accomplishment for having gotten through all these exercises.

Principals are worth the efforts, and they will benefit from the exercises. Superintendents will benefit also, and most important, so will all of their students.

Appendix A

THE DATA LIST

Data derived from Chapter Two,
A Principal And His School: A Case Study

School Description:

1. Name: The International School
2. Location: Somewhere in North America
3. Grades: Kindergarten through Grade Eight
4. Enrollment: Two Hundred Students
5. Staff:

   (a) Eleven Regular Classroom Teachers
   (b) One Reading Specialist
   (c) One Resource Teacher
   (d) One Assistant Principal
   (e) One Principal/Chief Administrator
   (f) Two Secretaries
   (g) Eight Parent Volunteer Classroom Aids

   (Class size/staff size equals the average of similar schools.)

6. The school was built to serve children of families associated with an international water reclamation project.
7. The school operates under contract to a private corporation.
8. The principal is a major shareholder of the corporation.
9. The school is seven years old.
10. Most students stay two years, a few stay three years, and only two or three students stay four years, none longer.

11. Fifty percent of the students are American, the others are from more than a dozen nations (most come from European and Middle Eastern countries).

12. Parents are responsible for student transportation.

13. The contract requires a mainstream U.S. public school program for all students.

14. Students are expected to make their normal gains in performance and achievement while attending the school.

15. The school goals are understood and accepted by the staff and community.

16. The school program emphasizes basic skills and academics.

17. Art, music, and physical education instruction are conducted by the regular classroom teachers.

18. No shop, homemaking, typing or similar courses exist.

19. No standardized testing program is in place.

20. Student progress is assessed by teacher and principal observation in all curriculum areas.

21. The principal has agreed to use standardized tests of basic skills, in the future, and only with the American students.

22. The school has a twenty station computer lab.

23. Computer software is acquired from the public domain at little or no cost.

24. The third and fifth grade teachers use the computer lab according to their own interests.

25. No current plan exists to integrate the computer lab into the regular program.

26. The school needs playground and physical education equipment.

27. The school has adequate instructional supplies and materials.

28. Staff members conduct some after-school programs for students.

29. The school atmosphere reflects high levels of cooperation at both the student and staff levels.

30. Students appear to be above grade in their basic language and math skills, and in most academic courses.

31. Student achievement in science (grades seven and eight) appears to be below school standards.

32. No conflict between students of any age group is apparent.

33. The school has not had a serious student or staff member accident.

34. Minor student accidents (bumps and bruises) are at a minimal level.

35. Students appear to be working hard at their studies.

36. All students are capable of working in a regular school program.

37. Staff members appear to be working hard at their jobs.

38. Staff members are provided annual in-service education.

39. All school personnel act friendly toward each other and towards visitors.

40. An unqualified teacher teaches upper grade science.

41. Staff members appear to respect the principal.

42. Staff members do not take their complaints to the principal.

43. Some staff members complain privately about a work overload.

44. Forty-seven percent of the professional staff, including the principal, are members of the same small religious sect.

45. An acknowledged incompetent teacher was allowed to remain in the classroom for an entire school year without being re-assigned or dismissed.

46. Recruiting teachers for the school is difficult.

47. The principal has expensive computer and television equipment in his office for his own use.

48. The principal reports a small contingency reserve.

49. Tuition costs are at the ninetieth percentile of similar contract schools.

50. Tuition is paid by each parent's employer.

51. No employer has complained about tuition rates or refused or delayed payment.

52. The principal's residence is supported out of school funds in accordance with the school contract.

53. The principal reports that he has saved the school thousands of operating dollars because of his frugality.

Community Description

54. The community is composed of water specialists and their families, including scientists, technicians, and laborers.

55. The great majority of parents are openly supportive of the school although they do want:

    55.1 A regular standardized testing program for American students

    55.2 An advisory group to review the school budget

56. The principal's home is one of the two best houses in the community.

57. A small group of parents have formally complained about:

57.1 Religious imbalance of the staff

57.2 An unqualified upper grade science teacher

57.3 Inadequate PE equipment

57.4 Inadequate after school programs for students

57.5 Failure to dismiss an incompetent teacher midyear due to poor budgeting for contingencies (such as hiring a replacement)

57.6 Excessive funds used to support the principal's residence

Principal Description

58. Credentialed English teacher and school administrator
59. "Thoreau-like" personality (self-existing), limited social skills
60. Considered unapproachable by staff
61. Regards himself as the local expert on school priorities
62. Has no close friends
63. Hard worker
64. Poor personnel recruiting skills (relies on staff members to recruit their friends)
65. Careful of money to the point of being penurious
66. Devotee of Mastery Learning
67. Experienced in nonstandard and overseas school operation and management
68. Asks for advice from those he respects, does not want unsolicited advice
69. Strong dislike for criticism, reduces school complaints to personality defects in the critic
70. Justifies his actions as being appropriate to his contract

Appendix B

Outcomes Useful to a Results-Based Principal Evaluation System

Results: The School Gets Results

1. parent complaints
2. student complaints
3. staff job satisfaction survey results
4. staff complaints
5. volunteer actions
6. student attendance records
7. staff attendance records
8. student awards
9. test scores
10. tallies, i.e., games won, number of participants
11. student grades
12. student survey results
13. parent survey results
14. elective course choices
15. library records
16. vandalism records
17. donation records
18. student council minutes
19. staff transfer requests - in
20. staff transfer requests - out
21. parent requests to transfer child - in
22. parent requests to transfer child - out
23. staff exit interviews
24. graduate follow-up reports
25. employee union bulletins
26. staff awards
27. budgets
28. financial reports

Safety: The School Is Safe

1. parent complaints
2. student complaints
29. maintenance order summary reports
30. equipment repair order summary reports
31. safety inspection reports of buildings
32. safety inspection reports of playground equipment
33. safety inspection reports of playground surfaces
34. accident reports
35. accident analysis reports
36. building health inspection reports for cleanliness
37. cafeteria health inspection reports
38. school nurse reports
39. school expenditure reports for items related to health and safety
40. fire marshal's reports
41. accident and injury claims
42. insurance company reports
43. lawsuits lost
44. lawsuits settled by insurance carrier
45. awards
46. letters of recognition and commendation
47. workman compensation claims
48. student cumulative folders
49. reports from other schools
50. guidance counselor records
51. discipline referral records
52. psychologist reports
53. nurse reports
54. suspension records
55. expulsion records
56. police notification records
57. parent reports
58. letters of appreciation
59. referrals from other government agencies
60. referrals from private practice physicians, psychologists
61. referrals from private sector agencies
62. citizen complaints
63. police bulletins
64. local newspapers
65. student complaints
66. citizen reports

Goals: The School Has Clear and Accepted Purposes

3. staff job satisfaction surveys, i.e., Purdue Opinionaire
4. staff complaints
6. student attendance records
7. staff work attendance records
58. letters of appreciation
67. staff memos from the principal
68. principal reports to district offices
69. principal bulletins to parents
70. personnel evaluation records
71. direct observation records
72. parent surveys
73. student surveys
74. expenditures analysis (do purchases reflect goals?)
75. staff requests for materials and equipment
76. grievance records
77. staff conference requests
78. volunteer actions (who participates in which activities)
79. staff attendance at extra-curricular activities
80. student awards
81. parent comments
82. student activities reports
83. resource speaker records
84. field trip records
85. staff awards
86. budgets
87. financial reports

Work: The People Are at Work

1. parent complaints
2. student complaints
3. staff job satisfaction surveys
4. staff complaints
6. student attendance records
7. staff work attendance records

31& 32. health and safety inspection reports

33. safety inspection reports of playground surfaces
51. discipline referral records
58. letters of appreciation
70. personnel evaluation records
71. direct observation records
88. school bulletins
89. parent bulletins
90. supervisors reports
91. guidance reports
92. district division head reports
93. consultant reports
94. staff exit interviews

Principal: The Principal Is a District Statesman

71. direct observations
95. principal initiated contacts
96. financial audits
97. union complaints
98. community inputs
99. principal-written communications
100. informal communication with the superintendent, from any source

Appendix C

A Sample List of Performance Objectives for School Principals

Leadership

I a. Leadership/Goal Orientation:

001 is task/achievement-oriented
002 establishes a climate of "task orientation" to all work stations
003 communicates school goals in clear and unambiguous language
004 gains widespread community support for school goals
005 gains widespread staff support for school goals
006 focuses staff energies on goal related problems
007 establishes and maintains high standards of performance for students and staff
008 establishes and carries out multiple programs for recognizing and rewarding good student work
009 incorporates special characteristics of the community into the student award and recognition programs
010 establishes and carries out multiple programs for recognizing and rewarding good staff work
011 incorporates special characteristics of the community into the staff recognition programs
012 will sacrifice a degree of personal popularity for the sake of students education
013 focuses personal energies on goal related problems
014 promotes staff participation in making program decisions

I b. Leadership/Communicator:

015 is clear and unambiguous about school goals
016 communicates in writing with clarity
017 communicates orally with clarity

018 maintains communicative contacts with appropriate audiences
019 enlists the active support of parents for program improvements
020 effectively communicates school goals and priorities to the community
021 conducts regular and frequent staff meetings
022 makes effective use of person to person and informal communication methods
023 conducts daily informal communications with students, staff, and community
024 establishes and maintains an effective formal internal communication system
025 utilizes personal communication with individual parents related to individual student need
026 conducts and/or arranges for school/community meetings

I c. Leadership/Style:

027 functions as instructional leader
028 promotes positive, friendly, and cooperative working relationships
029 promotes mutual trust and respect among staff
030 utilizes vested authority to maintain a well disciplined campus
031 relies on rational processes to exercise authority in typical situations vs. use of vested authority
032 retains vested authority of position, delegates only the authority required to accomplish work
033 does not trade authority as a solution to a problem
034 committed to rational debate and decision making
035 willingly collaborates in rational problem solving
036 promotes and assists the parent/school organization
037 promotes and participates in staff social activities
038 delegates authority and decision-making responsibilities appropriate to tasks and assignments
039 is actively involved with the school community
040 maintains an environment of steady and continuous change in the school program
041 executes role consistent with district philosophy
042 executes role consistent with district governance

Management Functions

II a. Management Function/Planning

Priorities:
043 achievement and happiness of students is first priority
044 planning is consistent with district and community goals
045 establishes priorities among teachers' objectives consistent with school priorities
046 executes planning and budgeting functions in a thorough and timely manner
047 seeks and utilizes staff advice on important issues

048 conducts systematic needs assessment to determine special needs of students

049 involves teachers in school planning in a peer relationship

050 actively involved in curriculum and instructional decisions in the school

Resources:

051 utilizes and allocates resources according to program priorities

052 develops plans within the constraints of available resources

053 utilizes district and external resources in developing school program

054 provides necessary materials and equipment to staff

055 provides classrooms with adequate and readily available materials and resources

056 makes effective use of district resources for program improvements

057 makes intelligent choices allocating funds and other school resources

II b. Management Function/Organizing

Time Management:

058 establishes effective framework for program innovation

059 executes organizing functions in a thorough and timely manner according to district guidelines

060 establishes procedures that reduce staff and student work interruptions

061 arranges schedules to afford necessary non-teaching time for staff members

062 conducts routine administrative matters without undo disruptions and in a quick efficient manner

Staffing:

063 executes staffing functions according to student needs and within the district guidelines

064 actively involved in teacher selection and assignment within the school

065 knowledgeable of teachers' individual abilities, competencies, and strengths

066 assigns staff according teachers' individual abilities, competencies, and strengths

067 assigns staff according to student needs

068 makes effective use of district consultive services

069 selects and assigns staff members to school projects to insure competent internal leadership

070 gathers and uses background data during personnel selection process

071 becomes knowledgeable of individual teacher values and expectations

II c. Management Function/Supervision

Supervision:

072 supports individual initiative consistent with school goals and priorities

073 clarifies staff members role and job performance expectations

074 promotes a friendly working environment

075 establishes a climate of "productivity" at all work stations

076 supervises staff to insure work is performed according to adopted procedures and specifications

077 establishes a cooperative and helpful work climate
078 clarifies teacher objectives and avoids ambiguity
079 is available and accessible to staff
080 reviews and ratifies teacher's instructional plans
081 establishes and executes procedures for staff supervision in accordance with district guidelines
082 monitors staff to insure utilization of feedback data
083 participates in teacher in-service programs
084 works directly with teachers on problems identified during classroom observations
085 visits teachers regularly and frequently
086 provides direct assistance to teachers with classroom problems

Evaluation:

087 executes the district staff evaluation program
088 conducts personnel evaluations with the aim of professional growth and program improvement
089 keeps all necessary records attenuate to personnel evaluation
090 carefully documents all summative judgments in the personnel evaluation process
091 effectively influences staff members in selecting and setting goals for their own growth
092 conducts personnel evaluations in an open and forthright manner

Directing:

093 influences teacher instructional strategies
094 influences cooperative teacher - pupil relationships in the classroom
095 influences the amount of classroom time devoted to instruction
096 influences teachers' program priorities and time allocation
097 influences classroom discipline
098 provides a structured in-service program for staff
099 provides an effective orientation program for new staff members
100 provides staff members with time management assistance
101 conducts staff in-service in areas of personal expertise

II d. Management Function/Controlling

Safety:

102 establishes an operates an effective building and equipment maintenance surveillance plan
103 insures the cleanliness of school facilities in accordance with district standards
104 establishes procedures and processes that insure student safety
105 effectively monitors staff behavior to protect students from physical and/or psychological abuse
106 establishes and enforces appropriate regulations to insure non-interference of school operations by disruptive community elements
107 effectively supervises schools' physical environment to enhance teaching and study
108 establishes procedures that insure neat and orderly work stations

109 establishes effective procedures for dealing with legal obligations of school, staff, students

110 establishes effective procedures for dealing with emergencies

111 conducts daily surveillance of campus

Discipline:

112 establishes effective student discipline procedures

113 involved in supporting teachers classroom discipline program

114 monitors classroom interpersonal relationships and supports teachers' classroom control measures

115 establishes effective procedures for out of classroom discipline problems

Feedback:

116 regularly and systematically gathers quantitative data which reflects student achievement and progress

117 regularly records and reports special achievements and/or recognitions of students

118 establishes and carries on a process of continuous data collection related to student performance

119 monitors student progress closely

120 makes effective use of student test scores in making program improvements and staff in-service

121 regularly and systematically gathers quantitative data which reflects staff achievements and progress

122 regularly records and reports special achievements and/or recognitions of staff

123 communicates information regarding staff and student accomplishments to the district in a clear and timely manner

124 provides staff with adequate feedback information regarding school achievement relative to goals

125 establishes and monitors effective reports of student progress between teachers and parents

126 provides continuous feedback information to students, staff, and community regarding school and student progress

127 establishes data collection processes that result in a minimum of obtrusions

128 provides accurate and timely feedback to district relative to the success or deficiencies of district functions

129 manages school budgets skillfully and with prudence

Knowledge

III a. Knowledge of Learning Theory

130 demonstrates knowledge of learning theory and applies this knowledge in assisting staff

131 works directly with staff on meeting needs of problem children

132 establishes effective guidance screening procedures

III b. Knowledge of Instruction

133 demonstrates knowledge of sound instructional practice and applies this knowledge in assisting staff

134 provides opportunities for staff visits/interaction with others both within and without the school

III c. Knowledge of Curriculum

135 demonstrates knowledge of curriculum resources and applies this knowledge in assisting staff

136 coordinates program goals among teachers and grade levels to achieve a balanced curriculum

137 gains the support of peers and district staff for program innovations

138 actively and directly involved in formative stages of program development

139 supervises the school testing program for proper test selection and utilization

140 maintains adequate knowledge of curriculum content to afford effective supervision of staff

141 provides intramural and extracurricular programs appropriate to the student body

142 seeks out and promotes the use of new materials and techniques

III d. Knowledge of District Organization and Services

143 demonstrates knowledge of district organization and services and uses this knowledge in assisting staff, students and community

144 accepts mature and intelligent counsel and direction

III e. Knowledge of Statutes, District Policy, and Contracts

145 demonstrates knowledge of district policy, collective bargaining contracts, and state statutes adequate to the administrative position

146 demonstrates knowledge of district philosophy and goals

147 demonstrates knowledge of district governance and operation

III f. Knowledge of Self

Exhibits high level of self awareness in areas of:

148 conflict resolution

149 personal vanities

150 trusting relationships

151 power relationships

152 personal vulnerabilities

153 maintains a regular program of professional reading related to the school and its programs

154 maintains an ongoing dialogue with fellow principals and district staff regarding professional concerns

155 seeks mature and intelligent counsel

Personal Competencies

IV a. Personal/Honesty

156 **is honest, direct, and sincere**

157 **communicates honestly and accurately**

IV b. Personal/Self Confidence

158 **exhibits self confidence**

159 **does not compromise the integrity of the school by yielding to inappropriate pressuring**

160 **does not abandon a position in the face of threats**

IV c. Personal/Responsibility

161 **seeks responsibility**

162 **accepts responsibility**

IV d. Personal/Empathy

163 **exhibits empathy for people**

164 **assesses human behavior according to peoples' psychological make-up rather than arbitrary standards**

165 **exhibits compassion for human problems**

IV e. Personal/Tolerance

166 **tolerant of human differences**

167 **operates in an unprejudiced manner**

IV f. Personal/Vitality

168 **maintains sufficient energy for the job**

169 **maintains high spirits for the job**

IV g. Personal/Judgment

170 **exhibits sound judgment**

171 **makes rational judgments with careful consideration of consequences and implications**

172 **develops innovative uses of school resources in solving problems and carrying out programs**

173 **analyzes problems, situations, and conditions to explore and explain underlying relationships**

174 **anticipates problems and takes appropriate intervening action**